AFFIRMATIVE ACTION

Other books in the At Issue series:

AFFIRMATIVE ACTION

Leora Maltz, *Book Editor*

Bruce Glassman, *Vice President*
Bonnie Szumski, *Publisher*
Helen Cothran, *Managing Editor*

GREENHAVEN PRESS
An imprint of Thomson Gale, a part of The Thomson Corporation

Detroit • New York • San Francisco • San Diego • New Haven, Conn.
Waterville, Maine • London • Munich

© 2005 Thomson Gale, a part of The Thomson Corporation.

Thomson and Star Logo are trademarks and Gale and Greenhaven Press are registered trademarks used herein under license.

For more information, contact
Greenhaven Press
27500 Drake Rd.
Farmington Hills, MI 48331-3535
Or you can visit our Internet site at http://www.gale.com

LIBRARY OF CONGRESS CATALOGING-IN-PUBLICATION DATA

Affirmative action / Leora Maltz, book editor.
  p. cm. — (At issue)
Includes bibliographical references and index.
ISBN 0-7377-2002-6 (pbk. : alk. paper) —
ISBN 0-7377-2001-8 (lib. bdg. : alk. paper)
  1. Discrimination in higher education—United States. 2. Universities and colleges—United States—Admission. 3. Educational equalization—United States. 4. Affirmative action programs—United States. I. Maltz, Leora. II. At issue (San Diego, Calif.)
LC212.42.A37 2005
378.1'012—dc22
                                                2004042546

Printed in the United States of America

Contents

Introduction

Affirmative action is a product of the civil rights era, that time from the late 1950s through the 1960s when African Americans fought to live as equal citizens in the country of their birth. Under the leadership of Martin Luther King and organizations such as the National Association for the Advancement of Colored People, blacks in America waged a long campaign of passive resistance against the racism endemic to American society, using sit-ins, marches, and rallies. By the 1960s, despite the assassination of King and the deaths of many activists, some significant advances in civil rights had been made, particularly in the South: Schools and universities were actively desegregated, and public facilities were racially integrated. Affirmative action emerged during this difficult time, as a century after the official abolition of slavery, the U.S. government finally began to address the institutionalized racism that was still to be found throughout the country. Thus it was after extensive pressure from the civil rights movement that President John F. Kennedy enacted several important laws, including Executive Order 10925 in 1961, which stated that government contractors had to take "affirmative action to ensure that applicants are employed . . . without regard to race, creed, color or national origin."

But it was Kennedy's successor, President Lyndon B. Johnson, who was responsible for actually implementing most of the civil rights legislation, including the landmark Civil Rights Act of 1964, which barred all kinds of discrimination. Affirmative action was one of Johnson's Great Society initiatives, officially made into law in 1965 by Executive Order 11246, which required federal contractors to take affirmative action to ensure that persons of color were entitled to the same employment opportunities as whites. Thus it was in 1965, exactly one hundred years after the 1865 abolition of slavery, that the civil rights movement succeeded in producing a commitment from the U.S. government to actively include African Americans in America's elite educational institutions, boardrooms, and halls of political power.

Both Johnson and Kennedy conceived of affirmative action as applying primarily to employment practices, specifically to ensuring that government hiring practices were nondiscriminatory, but the idea and practice of affirmative action was soon adopted by U.S. colleges in an effort to redress their racial imbalances. Later the military and private business, similarly dominated by white males, also embraced affirmative action to varying degrees.

In the 1960s the standard explanation offered for affirmative action was that it sought to redress some of the social inequalities produced by slavery and its aftermath; affirmative action was thus specifically a policy aimed at equalizing a society in which blacks were dramatically underrepresented in numerous spheres. According to economist Alan Krueger, in 1969 the average black male in his thirties earned 37 percent less than his white male counterpart—a glaring income gap that was attributed largely to ongoing discrimination in education as well as commerce. Indeed, blacks generally occupied the lowest status, entry-level jobs in the economy while whites dominated the ranks of the elite. The establishment of affirmative action was thus based on a theory of redistributive justice. It also centered on the notion that the playing field of life was not level for all Americans but was dramatically tilted in favor of whites, and only an active program of redress such as affirmative action could help even it out. In his Howard University speech in 1965, President Johnson argued: "You do not take a man who for years has been hobbled by chains, liberate him, bring him to the starting line of a race, saying, 'You are free to compete with all the others,' and still justly believe you have been completely fair."

While it was indisputable that African Americans had suffered from centuries of slavery, soon other groups also claimed to be victims of white male patriarchy too: Women argued that they had been deprived of the vote and excluded from the workforce, and Hispanics said that they had been subject to job discrimination and exploitation as well as social biases. Native Americans, killed en masse by white settlers and driven from their lands, similarly claimed their right to a place in the institutions of American power and privilege. In the course of time, affirmative action policies were extended to these other minorities. Many viewed this expansion as problematic, for it changed affirmative action from being a specifically racial policy, aimed at redressing injustices against African Americans, to being a policy with much broader and more ambitious aims. Defenders of affirmative action thus shifted from promoting racial integration to producing social diversity. Indeed, these days diversity (itself a debatable good) has become the most popular explanation for affirmative action.

Not everyone agrees with justifying affirmative action on the grounds of diversity. For example, University of California at Berkeley linguistics professor John McWhorter asserts that "the Supreme Court must strike down the use of 'diversity' as a coy, Orwellian euphemism for treating middle-class black students as lesser minds." However, others, such as University of Michigan at Ann Arbor president Lee Bollinger, firmly believe that diversity itself should be the fundamental goal of affirmative action because it helps students to understand life from the point of view of others. Diversity "is essential to learning because it helps students to understand the full complexity of life—to make the empathetic leap," Bollinger states. For better or for worse, so many people now associate affirmative action with diversity that the term *diversity* is frequently used as a shorthand for the notion of affirmative action itself.

As diversity emerged as the goal of affirmative action and the range of recipients of affirmative action expanded, certain whites increasingly felt themselves to be the victims of "reverse discrimination." It seemed to them that so many people were favored over them that having white skin had in fact become a drawback. This resentment has been responsible for most legal challenges to affirmative action, which have taken the form of lawsuits brought by white applicants rejected from elite colleges or graduate schools. The first complaint of this sort was filed by Allan Bakke against the University of California at Davis Medical School. It reached the Supreme Court in 1978, with the justices rendering a famous decision that endorsed the constitutionality of affirmative action—colleges and universities could consider race as a factor in their admissions decisions—while banning the use of actual quota systems. The landmark *Bakke* decision shaped affirmative action policies for twenty-five years in American higher education until the mid-1990s, when lawyers from the Center for Individual Rights, an organization committed to fighting affirmative action, shepherded two separate cases through the court system. Both cases were brought against the University of Michigan at Ann Arbor by several rejected white applicants. These plaintiffs, Jennifer Gratz and Barbara Grutter, argued that their lives had been irreparably damaged by affirmative action, which had denied them educational opportunities they had worked hard for and deserved. These plaintiffs felt affirmative action to be an unjust and unfair policy, as they personally had never kept slaves, lynched anyone, or consigned a black person to the back of the bus.

The two cases brought against the University of Michigan went before the Supreme Court in 2003, with judgments being rendered in June of that year. In the lead-up to the trial, while the Supreme Court wrestled with the future of affirmative action, its pros and cons were being argued with renewed vigor in newspapers, on radio, on TV, and on Internet bulletin boards. Finally the justices emerged from chambers, deeply divided, with a series of decisions that reflected the complexity and confusion surrounding the issue. They ruled against the University of Michigan in *Gratz v. Bollinger*, deciding that the use of quotas for race by the undergraduate admissions office was unconstitutional. Trial evidence showed that minority undergraduate applicants to the University of Michigan were awarded twenty points out of a total of 140. Moreover, because the admissions system handled thousands of applications, it had to rely on a fairly simplistic formula to weigh race as a factor without giving sufficient consideration to each applicant's individual circumstances. However, in the case brought against the University of Michigan Law School by rejected applicant Barbara Grutter (*Grutter v. Bollinger*), the Supreme Court justices upheld the law school admissions processes as fair and constitutional.

The debate over the justice of affirmative action policies is far from over. Indeed, the controversial June 2003 Supreme Court decisions have only reignited the issue, sparking debate and commentary from many quarters. The authors in *At Issue: Affirmative Action* examine the key arguments for and against affirmative action that have been made in the last few years. Some argue passionately for the merits of affirmative action while others insist it must be abolished.

1

Affirmative Action: An Overview

David C. Slade

David C. Slade is an attorney who has been a member of the Supreme Court bar since 1986. He practices law in Bowie, Maryland.

Affirmative action policies are largely a result of America's tragic history of slavery. Indeed, in 1863, when slaves were finally freed, President Abraham Lincoln envisioned black children entering the educational system that was already in place for whites. However, racism in the South prevented such equalized or integrated education from ever being realized. A major victory of the civil rights era of the 1960s was thus the implementation of affirmative action programs in education to ensure that children of all races could receive a similar education. By 1973 some white college applicants began to feel they were being discriminated against. One such person, Allan Bakke, sued the University of California Medical School in a famous case that landed before the Supreme Court, which ruled that colleges could use race as one of several factors in admissions decisions. Thirty years later, this perception of "reverse discrimination" remains strong among some whites, as evidenced by a suit filed against the University of Michigan for its admissions policies.

When Barbara Grutter received a letter from the University of Michigan Law School denying her admission, the thought of Abraham Lincoln or the Civil War probably never entered her mind. But the bad news was a lingering legacy of the war; her denial was based largely on her race.

Affirmative action is the legacy of slavery

On New Year's Day, 1863, President Abraham Lincoln signed the Emancipation Proclamation, freeing the 3.12 million slaves living inside the rebellious Confederate states. Lincoln planned to bring Louisiana, with 17 of the 48 parishes held by federal forces, back into the Union. Writing to the military governor in 1864, he advised that Louisiana recognize the Eman-

David C. Slade, "Not So Black-and-White a Question," *World & I*, vol. 18, March 2003, p. 56.

cipation Proclamation, so that "the two races could gradually live themselves out of their old relation" and into a new era of coexistence. The key to Lincoln's plan? "Education for young blacks should be included in the plan." So it became that black children were admitted to Louisiana's public schools.

In April 1865, John Wilkes Booth killed Lincoln. His bullet also killed the president's benevolent vision of conciliatory reconstruction and peaceful coexistence between the races.

Andrew Johnson, the Tennessee "War" Democrat who assumed the presidency after Lincoln's assassination, carried a personal vengeance against the Confederacy. Although the Thirteenth Amendment abolishing slavery passed while Johnson was in the White House, a vengeful federal government imposed military rule over the former Confederate states. In response, the southern states systematically began to enact laws to separate the races in schools, eateries, parks, and even public transportation. The Jim Crow era had begun.

"Separate but equal" is not equal

In 1892 Homer Plessy, a 30-year-old black shoemaker, was jailed in Louisiana for sitting in a "white" railroad car. Four years later, the U.S. Supreme Court, in *Plessy v. Ferguson*, upheld the law as constitutional as long as the separate facilities were "equal." For the next six decades, this "separate but equal" ruling would be doctrine in American law, policy, and society.

But the words of Justice John Harlan, the lone dissenter in *Plessy*, were visionary when he wrote: "Our Constitution is color-blind, and neither knows nor tolerates classes among citizens. In respect of civil rights, all citizens are equal before the law. . . . In my opinion, the judgment this day rendered will . . . defeat the beneficent purposes which the people of the United States had in view when they adopted the recent amendments of the Constitution." Thus did Harlan echo Lincoln's benevolent hopes.

Harlan's views finally prevailed in 1954, when the Supreme Court expressly overruled *Plessy*, clearly holding in *Brown v. Board of Education* that "separate educational facilities are inherently unequal." With this clear signal from the Court, many colleges and universities instituted special admissions policies designed to assist "disadvantaged" students, such as blacks and Native Americans. But what was heralded as progressive policy was soon struck down by the Supreme Court as reverse discrimination.

The *Bakke* precedent

In 1973 and '74, Allan Bakke applied to the University of California Medical School. The school had two admissions tracks, one for regular and one for minority group applicants. Regular applicants had to have a GPA of 2.5 or higher. Minority applicants, however, weren't held to the 2.5 cutoff; nor were they ranked against regular applicants. Sixteen out of 100 slots were held solely for minority applicants.

Bakke, a regular applicant with a GPA above 2.5 and test scores significantly higher than those of most minority students, was rejected twice. In both years the 84 regular slots had been filled by applicants with better scores than Bakke's, and the 16 minority slots had been filled with students with GPAs of less than 2.5 and worse test scores. Bakke sued, arguing that he was excluded based solely on his race, in violation of the Fourteenth Amendment's equal protection clause.

In one of the most fractured and splintered plurality decisions it has ever handed down, the Supreme Court agreed with Bakke, noting that "white applicants could compete only for 84 seats in the entering class, rather than the 100 open to minority applicants," a distinction based solely on race and ethnic status. Because the admission policy discriminated solely on race, the Court held the program unconstitutional. But *Bakke* did not prohibit universities from considering an applicant's race as one of many factors—just not as the sole factor.

Although the decision is confused, it is out of *Bakke* that our present-day affirmative action programs arose. Race is just one of several factors that colleges and universities can use to try to remedy past discrimination and bring racial and ethnic diversity to the student body.

Following *Bakke*, the University of Michigan School of Law drafted its admissions policy in 1992. In addition to a candidate's scholastic record, his (or her) race and ethnic background was taken into account. The policy's stated goal was to have a critical mass of at least 10 percent minority students in each entering class.

Grutter sues the University of Michigan

The race factor cut against Grutter, a white candidate. Finding out the school had accepted numerous minority students with lower grades than herself, she sued, arguing she had been discriminated against precisely because of her race.

Although the law school did not set a quota as in *Bakke*, at trial it was statistically demonstrated that the affirmative action policy resulted in far more minority students being admitted without race as a factor. Without considering race, only 4 to 10 percent of minority students would be admitted; under the school's affirmative action policy, the percentage rose to 26 to 35 percent. The judge held that the admissions policy was "practically indistinguishable from a quota system" and struck down the policy as unconstitutional. But the Sixth Circuit Court of Appeals reversed, holding that the law school's compelling interest in a diverse student body justified its race-based admissions policy.

After winning at trial, then losing on appeal, Grutter is now taking her case to the Supreme Court [she lost the case]. With colleges and universities throughout the nation having much the same admissions policies as Michigan, and with the circuit courts in disarray after *Bakke*, the Supreme Court agreed to hear the case. Perhaps the Court can, at last, provide a clear answer to Lincoln's quandary of how to remedy past discrimination in a land where the Constitution is color-blind and all citizens are equal before the law.

2

Affirmative Action Helps Minorities

Charles J. Ogletree Jr.

Charles J. Ogletree Jr. is a professor at Harvard Law School. He is also a member of the Stanford Board of Trustees.

Affirmative action may not be a perfect system, but there should be no doubt that it has engendered many successes. It has opened the doors of America's most elite educational institutions to minority students, granting them unprecedented opportunities. Although minorities may have been admitted to highly competitive universities such as Stanford under affirmative action outreach programs, once enrolled, they have had to compete on an equal footing with whites. The overwhelming successes of so many of the minority students admitted under affirmative action programs of the 1960s and 1970s testifies to the extent that affirmative action has benefited minority individuals.

My dreams became reality as a result of my Stanford education. My father, who grew up in Birmingham, Ala., and my mother, a native of Little Rock, Ark., never finished high school. They grew up in a segregated South that offered few opportunities and many obstacles for African Americans. I grew up in Merced, Calif., in an environment where many of my peers viewed merely staying alive and getting a job as a successful course in life. But, with a push from my parents, I was determined to be the first in my family to attend college. With help from high school counselors, I discovered Stanford. And thanks to an aggressive minority outreach program by the admissions office, I was given the opportunity of a first-rate education. Without affirmative action, I would never have applied to, and certainly would not have attended, Stanford.

We must keep affirmative action—and keep refining it. It is a small but significant way to compensate victims of slavery, Jim Crow [discriminatory] laws, discrimination and immigration restrictions. It is also a means to assure that institutions such as Stanford will celebrate and foster that which they simply cannot avoid: diversity in a democratic society. Affirmative action admissions policies seek to realign the balance of

Charles J. Ogletree Jr., "The Case for Affirmative Action," *Stanford Alumni Magazine*, September/October 1996. Copyright © 1996 by the Stanford Alumni Association. Reproduced by permission.

power and opportunity by doing what is, at heart, quite simple: affirmatively including the formerly excluded.

There are critics of affirmative action who claim it is no longer needed, or unfairly discriminates "in reverse" or "stigmatizes" admitted minority students. I disagree.

We still need affirmative action

Those who claim affirmative action is no longer needed believe that the field has been leveled. But they ignore alarming figures. [In 1995], only 1,455 African Americans received PhDs in the United States. During the same year, 24,608 whites were awarded PhDs. The truth is that while America has made progress on racial issues, these changes are recent, vulnerable to being reversed and in fact nowhere near completed.

Those who cry "reverse discrimination" base their views almost exclusively on a belief that minority test scores are too low. But they fail to acknowledge that test scores and subsequent performance in college have a correlation that is, to say the least, inexact. When we insist on test scores as an ultimate measure of merit, we exclude, once again, students who have not had access to good public education or to funds that pay for preparatory courses for those tests. We exclude those who, given the opportunity, will display their ability.

The majority of minorities strongly favor affirmative action because of the benefits and opportunities it affords.

Finally, those who would eradicate affirmative action because it "stigmatizes" minorities have two flaws in their argument. Stigma is the product of racist attitudes that still persist today. As a result, killing affirmative action would do little, probably nothing, to ameliorate the stigmatization of minorities. Indeed, one wonders, even for the few whom affirmative action might arguably stigmatize: Would they feel better and achieve more being excluded from a good education entirely? That question ties into the second flaw in the "stigmatization" argument: Opponents rely on the exceptional case, not the rule. (Just as they tend to point the minuscule number of failures rather than the many successes.) The majority of minorities strongly favor affirmative action because of the benefits and opportunities it affords.

I was attracted to Stanford precisely because of its affirmative action programs. Here was an institution that clearly recognized that some people enter life with different abilities and opportunities, and that standardized tests were not the only way to judge issues of character, creativity and intellectual promise. When I arrived on campus, I found there was no affirmative action in course selection or grading. I was expected to compete with my peers on an equal basis. I learned that success was not automatic. I got my bachelor's degree in three years and graduated with distinction. I spent my fourth year obtaining my master's degree, and giving serious thought to the next stages of life.

Affirmative action has been a success

The experiences of many of my minority classmates is a ringing endorsement of affirmative action. Most came from families where the parents had not gone to college, and many were from single-parent households. Moreover, many went on to become successful doctors, lawyers and business leaders, and others are prominent school teachers, public servants and entrepreneurs.

It is my hope that one day we will no longer need affirmative action. As our society becomes more diverse, the need for specific programs aimed at targeted groups will obviously diminish. However, that time has not yet arrived. My two teenage children, who are both college bound, are far better qualified to navigate the educational waters than I was 25 years ago. Despite this laudable progress, they are still judged in everyday life, by race. They are constantly reminded by comments, innuendo and circumstances of their ethnicity precisely because we have not been able as a society to overcome the issues of race.

The affirmative action policies promoted by Stanford recognize that, for more than 300 years, African Americans were treated differently because of their race. The important efforts over the course of the past 30 years by government and private institutions have gone a considerable distance in facing up to this history. It will not take 300 years, or even 100 years, to address the sad legacy of our nation's past. We have made a lot of progress. This is no time to turn back.

3

Affirmative Action Harms Minorities

Clarence Thomas

Clarence Thomas is a Supreme Court justice. Generally viewed as a conservative, he does not support affirmative action.

The admissions policies at the University of Michigan's Law School are unjust. Minorities do not need affirmative action, and little evidence exists to suggests it helps them. Affirmative action not only stigmatizes black people as being intellectually inferior, but evidence also suggests that it hurts minorities by failing to consider their needs. Minority students are not pushed to achieve as much as majority students under affirmative action policies, and they therefore do not score as highly on standardized tests, maintaining the myth of their inferiority. Moreover, when minority students are admitted to law schools for which they are not adequately prepared, it is the student, the so-called "beneficiary" of affirmative action, who is hurt.

Editor's note: In 2003 the U.S. Supreme Court decided to strike down the University of Michigan's undergraduate admissions affirmative action program in Gratz v. Bollinger *while upholding the graduate admissions program in* Grutter v. Bollinger.

[E]arly civil rights activist] Frederick Douglass, speaking to a group of abolitionists almost 140 years ago, delivered a message lost on today's majority:

> "In regard to the colored people, there is always more that is benevolent, I perceive, than just, manifested towards us. What I ask for the negro is not benevolence, not pity, not sympathy, but simply *justice*. The American people have always been anxious to know what they shall do with us. . . . I have had but one answer from the beginning. Do nothing with us! Your doing with us has already played the mischief with us. Do nothing with us! If the apples will not remain on

Clarence Thomas, opinion, *Barbara Grutter, Petitioner v. Lee Bollinger et al.*, U.S. Supreme Court, June 23, 2003.

the tree of their own strength, if they are worm-eaten at the core, if they are early ripe and disposed to fall, let them fall! . . . And if the negro cannot stand on his own legs, let him fall also. All I ask is, give him a chance to stand on his own legs! Let him alone! . . . Your interference is doing him positive injury." "What the Black Man Wants: An Address Delivered in Boston, Massachusetts, on 26 January 1865.". . .

Like Douglass, I believe blacks can achieve in every avenue of American life without the meddling of university administrators. Because I wish to see all students succeed whatever their color, I share, in some respect, the sympathies of those who sponsor the type of discrimination advanced by the University of Michigan Law School (Law School) [under its affirmative action admissions policies]. The Constitution does not, however, tolerate institutional devotion to the status quo in admissions policies when such devotion ripens into racial discrimination. Nor does the Constitution countenance the unprecedented deference the Court gives to the Law School, an approach inconsistent with the very concept of "strict scrutiny."

The Law School's policies are unjust

No one would argue that a university could set up a lower general admission standard and then impose heightened requirements only on black applicants. Similarly, a university may not maintain a high admission standard and grant exemptions to favored races. The Law School, of its own choosing, and for its own purposes, maintains an exclusionary admissions system that it knows produces racially disproportionate results. Racial discrimination is not a permissible solution to the self-inflicted wounds of this elitist admissions policy.

The majority upholds the Law School's racial discrimination not by interpreting the people's Constitution, but by responding to a faddish slogan of the cognoscenti. Nevertheless, I concur in part in the Court's opinion. First, I agree with the Court insofar as its decision, which approves of only one racial classification, confirms that further use of race in admissions remains unlawful. Second, I agree with the Court's holding that racial discrimination in higher education admissions will be illegal in 25 years. . . . I respectfully dissent from the remainder of the Court's opinion and the judgment, however, because I believe that the Law School's current use of race violates the Equal Protection Clause and that the Constitution means the same thing today as it will in 300 months. . . .

> *I believe blacks can achieve in every avenue of American life without the meddling of university administrators.*

The Constitution abhors classifications based on race, not only because those classifications can harm favored races or are based on illegitimate motives, but also because every time the government places citizens on racial registers and makes race relevant to the provision of burdens or benefits, it demeans us all. "Purchased at the price of immeasurable human suffering, the equal protection principle reflects our Nation's understanding that such classifications ultimately have a destructive impact on the individual and our society." *Adarand Construction, Inc. v. Peña.* . . .

Diversity does not benefit minorities

The Court's deference to the Law School's conclusion that its racial experimentation leads to educational benefits will, if adhered to, have serious collateral consequences. The Court relies heavily on social science evidence to justify its deference. . . . The Court never acknowledges, however, the growing evidence that racial (and other sorts of) heterogeneity actually impairs learning among black students. See, *e.g.,* Flower & Pascarella, *Cognitive Effects of College Racial Composition on African American Students After 3 Years of College*, 40 J. of *College Student Development* 669, 674 (1999) (concluding that black students experience superior cognitive development at Historically Black Colleges (HBCs) and that, even among blacks, "a substantial diversity moderates the cognitive effects of attending an HBC"); Allen, *The Color of Success: African-American College Student Outcomes at Predominantly White and Historically Black Public Colleges and Universities*, 62 Harv. Educ. Rev. 26, 35 (1992) (finding that black students attending HBCs report higher academic achievement than those attending predominantly white colleges).

> *"[Race] classifications . . . have a destructive impact on the individual and our society."*

At oral argument in *Gratz v. Bollinger,* . . . counsel for respondents stated that "most every single one of [the HBCs] do have diverse student bodies." . . . What precisely counsel meant by "diverse" is indeterminate, but it is reported that in 2000 at Morehouse College, one of the most distinguished HBC's in the Nation, only 0.1% of the student body was white, and only 0.2% was Hispanic. College Admissions Data Handbook 2002–2003, p. 613 (43d ed. 2002) (hereinafter College Admissions Data Handbook). And at Mississippi Valley State University, a public HBC, only 1.1% of the freshman class in 2001 was white. . . . If there is a "critical mass" of whites at these institutions, then "critical mass" is indeed a very small proportion.

The majority grants deference to the Law School's "assessment that diversity will, in fact, yield educational benefit." It follows, therefore, that an HBC's assessment that racial homogeneity will yield educational benefits would similarly be given deference. An HBC's rejection of white applicants in order to maintain racial homogeneity seems permissible, therefore, under the majority's view of the Equal Protection Clause. But see *United States v. Fordice* . . . ("Obviously, a State cannot maintain . . . traditions by closing particular institutions, historically white or historically black, to particular racial groups"). Contained within today's majority opinion is the seed of a new constitutional justification for a concept I thought long and rightly rejected—racial segregation. . . .

Affirmative action harms minorities

The absence of any articulated legal principle supporting the majority's principal holding suggests another rationale. I believe what lies beneath the Court's decision today are the benighted notions that one can tell when racial discrimination benefits (rather than hurts) minority groups, . . . and that racial discrimination is necessary to remedy general societal ills. This Court's precedents supposedly settled both issues, but clearly the majority still cannot commit to the principle that racial classifications are *per se* harmful and that almost no amount of benefit in the eye of the beholder can justify such classifications.

Putting aside what I take to be the Court's implicit rejection of *Adarand's* holding that beneficial and burdensome racial classifications are equally invalid, I must contest the notion that the Law School's discrimination benefits those admitted as a result of it. The Court spends considerable time discussing the impressive display of *amicus* support for the Law School in this case from all corners of society. . . . But nowhere in any of the filings in this Court is any evidence that the purported "beneficiaries" of this racial discrimination prove themselves by performing at (or even near) the same level as those students who receive no preferences. . . .

The silence in this case is deafening to those of us who view higher education's purpose as imparting knowledge and skills to students, rather than a communal, rubber-stamp, credentialing process. The Law School is not looking for those students who, despite a lower LSAT score or undergraduate grade point average, will succeed in the study of law. The Law School seeks only a facade—it is sufficient that the class looks right, even if it does not perform right.

Racial (and other sorts of) heterogeneity actually impairs learning among black students.

The Law School tantalizes unprepared students with the promise of a University of Michigan degree and all of the opportunities that it offers. These overmatched students take the bait, only to find that they cannot succeed in the cauldron of competition. And this mismatch crisis is not restricted to elite institutions. See T. Sowell, *Race and Culture* 176–177 (1994) ("Even if most minority students are able to meet the normal standards at the 'average' range of colleges and universities, the systematic mismatching of minority students begun at the top can mean that such students are generally overmatched throughout all levels of higher education"). Indeed, to cover the tracks of the aestheticists, this cruel farce of racial discrimination must continue—in selection for the *Michigan Law Review*, see University of Michigan Law School Student Handbook 2002–2003, pp. 39–40 (noting the presence of a "diversity plan" for admission to the review), and in hiring at law firms and for judicial clerkships—until the "beneficiaries" are no longer tolerated. While these students may graduate with law degrees, there is no evidence that they have received a qualitatively better legal education (or become better lawyers) than if they had gone to a less "elite" law school for which they were better prepared. And the aestheticists will never address the real problems facing "underrepresented minorities," instead continuing their social experiments on other people's children.

Affirmative action stigmatizes blacks

Beyond the harm the Law School's racial discrimination visits upon its test subjects, no social science has disproved the notion that this discrimination "engender[s] attitudes of superiority or, alternatively, provoke[s] resentment among those who believe that they have been wronged by the government's use of race." *Adarand.* . . . "These programs stamp minorities with a badge of inferiority and may cause them to develop dependencies or to adopt an attitude that they are 'entitled' to preferences." *Ibid.*

Racial classifications are per se *harmful.*

It is uncontested that each year, the Law School admits a handful of blacks who would be admitted in the absence of racial discrimination. . . . Who can differentiate between those who belong and those who do not? The majority of blacks are admitted to the Law School because of discrimination, and because of this policy all are tarred as undeserving. This problem of stigma does not depend on determinacy as to whether those stigmatized are actually the "beneficiaries" of racial discrimination. When blacks take positions in the highest places of government, industry, or academia, it is an open question today whether their skin color played a part in their advancement. The question itself is the stigma—because either racial discrimination did play a role, in which case the person may be deemed "otherwise unqualified," or it did not, in which case asking the question itself unfairly marks those blacks who would succeed without discrimination. Is this what the Court means by "visibly open"? . . .

The test scores gap is not shrinking

The Court also holds that racial discrimination in admissions should be given another 25 years before it is deemed no longer narrowly tailored to the Law School's fabricated compelling state interest. . . . While I agree that in 25 years the practices of the Law School will be illegal, they are, for the reasons I have given, illegal now. The majority does not and cannot rest its time limitation on any evidence that the gap in credentials between black and white students is shrinking or will be gone in that timeframe. In recent years there has been virtually no change, for example, in the proportion of law school applicants with LSAT scores of 165 and higher who are black. In 1993 blacks constituted 1.1% of law school applicants in that score range, though they represented 11.1% of all applicants. . . . In 2000 the comparable numbers were 1.0% and 11.3%. . . . No one can seriously contend, and the Court does not, that the racial gap in academic credentials will disappear in 25 years. Nor is the Court's holding that racial discrimination will be unconstitutional in 25 years made contingent on the gap closing in that time.

Indeed, the very existence of racial discrimination of the type practiced by the Law School may impede the narrowing of the LSAT testing gap. An applicant's LSAT score can improve dramatically with preparation, but such preparation is a cost, and there must be sufficient benefits attached to an improved score to justify additional study. Whites scoring between 163 and 167 on the LSAT are routinely rejected by the Law School, and thus whites aspiring to admission at the Law School have every incentive to improve their score to levels above that range. . . . Blacks, on the other hand, are nearly guaranteed admission if they score above 155. . . . As admission prospects approach certainty, there is no incentive for the black applicant to continue to prepare for the LSAT once he is reasonably assured of achieving the requisite score. It is far from certain that the LSAT test-taker's behavior is responsive to the Law School's admissions policies. Nevertheless, the possibility remains that this racial discrimination will help fulfill the bigot's prophecy about black underperformance—just as it confirms the conspiracy theorist's belief that "institutional racism" is at fault for every racial disparity in our society. . . .

For the immediate future, however, the majority has placed its *imprimatur* on a practice that can only weaken the principle of equality embodied in the Declaration of Independence and the Equal Protection Clause. "Our Constitution is color-blind, and neither knows nor tolerates classes among citizens." *Plessy v. Ferguson.* . . . It has been nearly 140 years since Frederick Douglass asked the intellectual ancestors of the Law School to "do nothing with us!" and the Nation adopted the Fourteenth Amendment. Now we must wait another 25 years to see this principle of equality vindicated. I therefore respectfully dissent from the remainder of the Court's opinion and the judgment.

4

Affirmative Action Encourages Diversity

Commonweal

Commonweal *magazine is a biweekly review of politics, religion, and culture. Founded in 1924, it is edited by Catholic laypeople and focuses especially on ethical issues in U.S. society and international affairs.*

Affirmative action encourages diversity, bringing together people of both sexes and many different racial, ethnic, and religious backgrounds in the educational system and in the workplace. In fact, affirmative action has so long been associated with its goal—diversity—that the two concepts are often employed interchangeably. Claims that the sole goal of America's public colleges is to provide the means to individual advancement are faulty; universities have a moral obligation to serve all groups within the society.

I s affirmative action the victim of its own success? That's one conclusion to be drawn from *Gratz v. Bollinger* and *Grutter v. Bollinger*, two cases challenging affirmative-action policies at the University of Michigan.[1] Affirmative action has always counterposed two basic aspects of the American notion of equal opportunity. Opponents argue that taking race or gender into account in hiring or university admissions is discrimination pure and simple. Proponents counter that taking such characteristics into account redresses a legacy of discrimination; in effect, affirmative-action programs create a level playing field where certain groups historically have been denied the opportunity to compete. Legally, affirmative action has barely survived scrutiny, and is far from assured of a future under the Rehnquist Supreme Court. Yet over the last thirty-five years accumulating evidence demonstrates that sociologically and economically affirmative-action programs have played an indispensable role in the emergence of a new black middle class and in opening doors to women in the university, the professions, and the corporate world.

The two cases involving the University of Michigan challenge the le-

---

1. The Supreme Court ruled in favor of Gratz but against Grutter in the summer of 2003.

Commonweal, "Diversity Dilemma," vol. 128, March 9, 2001, p. 5. Copyright © 2001 by the Commonweal Foundation. Reproduced by permission.

gality of the university's undergraduate admissions policies as well as those of the law school. Both actions against the university are being funded by the Center for Individual Rights, a Washington, D.C.–based public-interest law firm determined to dismantle race-based preferences. The suits have been called the Alamo of affirmative action, and the most important race cases in a generation. In response, the University of Michigan has mounted a comprehensive legal defense of affirmative action, at least as the university practices it.

Diversity benefits education, business, and government

Trial testimony documents the fact that racial and ethnic diversity in the classroom improves the critical thinking skills and intellectual motivation of all students. Further, students who attend schools with diverse populations are more likely to later settle in heterogeneous communities and to be active in improving those communities. Businesses, once opponents, now say they have benefited from affirmative action in higher education: twenty Fortune 500 companies, including Microsoft, General Mills, Texaco, Intel, Lucent Technologies, and Eli Lilly, submitted a brief in support of Michigan's undergraduate admissions procedures. The brief asserts that diversity in higher education is so vital to the companies' efforts "to hire and maintain a diverse work force" and to employ people "who have been educated in a diverse environment" that the government has a compelling interest in allowing public colleges to continue using affirmative action in admissions. The university won its case on undergraduate admissions in federal district court in December [2000].

Affirmative action has become synonymous with diversity

The *Gratz* and *Grutter* cases are noteworthy and controversial for other reasons, however, reasons that go beyond the classic justification for affirmative action as a remedy for historical and legal discrimination, most notably against African Americans. The new justifications invoked in the Michigan cases rest on the benefits that have come from affirmative action now defined as "diversity" broadly understood. The Supreme Court in *Bakke* (1978) paved the way for this development when it ruled that colleges and universities could use race as one factor in selecting students. Other factors have since emerged. Initially, the University of Michigan adopted affirmative action in an effort to provide an admissions boost to groups who had previously faced barriers in education and employment. Now the university defends its admissions policy to promote the benefits of diversity in the student body.

For some affirmative-action supporters, the evolution toward diversity is problematic. Won't the goal of providing opportunity to injured groups be obscured? If diversity is the good to be achieved, why not expand affirmative action to include Pakistanis, Norwegians, Arabs? Should recent immigrants benefit from affirmative-action programs originally designed to help black Americans? Certainly affirmative-action opponents think the d-word opens a Pandora's box of racial and ethnic gerrymandering. The plaintiff in the pending suit against the University of

Michigan Law School, for example, is an older, so-called "nontraditional" woman applicant. Might not she bring diversity benefits to the classroom too? Put on the waiting list at the law school, she argues that her scores and grades would have earned her admission had she been a member of a minority group.

One way for the university to address these questions is to voluntarily and periodically review its admissions policies in light of new demographic data, new sociological studies of affirmative action's impact, and the current debates on affirmative-action trends. This information is vital to the university's continual refinement of its goals in embracing affirmative action.

What is really at stake in these cases, however, is not the meaning of the term diversity, but the purpose of a university. In the plaintiffs' view, higher education is a means to individual advancement: therefore admissions must be strictly meritocratic (a notoriously amorphous standard itself). Scores and grades, they argue, are the only things that should count. The university sees its mission in a broader context. Yes, it must train scholars and contribute to the expansion of knowledge. But a public university also has social and moral obligations. Extending the benefits of education to all groups within society is one such obligation. If the studies showing the success of affirmative action are reliable, the extension of those benefits will not compromise the academic integrity of the institution, but will actually contribute to its improvement.

5

Diversity Should Not Be Legislated by Affirmative Action

Peter H. Schuck

Peter H. Schuck is a professor at Yale Law School. In his landmark book Diversity in America: Keeping Government at a Safe Distance, *he analyzes the history of diversity in the United States and how it has changed over time.*

Although fostering diversity may be an important goal for American institutions, diversity should not be legislated by publicly funded affirmative action programs. If private institutions subscribe to affirmative action programs, they express their own individual beliefs, and they should be permitted to retain this right of individual expression. However, public, state-run university systems are supposed to express the views of the public, and it is thus extremely problematic for them to mandate diversity. Such mandates suggest that all Americans condone the grouping of people by race and view equal treatment and merit as secondary goals.

The Supreme Court recently heard arguments in two cases involving ethnic and racial preferences in admissions at the University of Michigan, with a decision expected in late June or early July [2003]. In a court long divided by 5-4 votes on many of its most important decisions, the outcome of these cases is anyone's guess. Indeed, the court could decide to strike down the plan for Michigan's undergraduate admissions, which is akin to a hard quota system, while upholding its law school's more nuanced, multifactored program.[1]

Reading the tea leaves is notoriously unreliable where the court is concerned, but three points can help put the Michigan cases in sharper focus. Colleges and universities planning for the aftermath of the deci-

---

1. This is in fact exactly what happened; the law school case, *Grutter v. Bollinger*, was upheld, while the undergraduate suit, *Gratz v. Bollinger*, was ruled unconstitutional.

sion—whatever it is—should carefully consider them. First, Michigan hopes to use the so-called diversity rationale to find a safe harbor protected by Justice Lewis F. Powell Jr.'s opinion in *Regents of the University of California v. Bakke*, which held that colleges could possibly use race as a "plus" factor if needed to create a diverse student body. This hope is probably in vain. Even if Justice Powell's opinion is an authoritative precedent, which I doubt, plans like Michigan's probably cannot satisfy his criteria for ethnic and racial preferences.

Powell's opinion will probably carry little or no weight with today's court. No other justice joined his opinion. His discussion of diversity was abstract and unnecessary to the decision in *Bakke*, so it will be easy for today's court to ignore. The lower courts have since split on what Powell meant and whether his decision matters. And the opposition to affirmative action, both on the court and in the country (even among some black people), has grown since 1978, when *Bakke* was decided. Moreover, even if Powell's opinion is an authoritative precedent, Michigan's plans—particularly the undergraduate one—probably are unconstitutional. They define diversity too narrowly and arbitrarily. Like most such plans, for example, they do not give preferred status to Arab students, members of fundamentalist Christian groups, Hindu people, or others who would diversify the student body no less than the black and Hispanic students preferred by Michigan. (The state did introduce some evidence claiming a relationship between ethnic and racial status and an enhanced learning environment, but that relationship is rather murky.)

A bonus or a quota

Then, too, the bonus points that Michigan's undergraduate plan awards to members of its favored minority groups amounts pretty much to a quota—as the court is likely to conclude. No wonder, then, that the law school opted for a more flexible approach that considers race and ethnicity as just one factor among many used in order to achieve what the school considers a "critical mass" of minority students. Still, it is understandable that Michigan has seized upon Powell's diversity rationale to defend its plans. After all, the only other justification for racial and ethnic preferences that the court has accepted—remedying the institution's own past discrimination—does not apply to Michigan, because it has no such history.

Michigan's plans—particularly the undergraduate one—probably are unconstitutional.

In addition, the diversity rationale is attractive because the very concept of diversity has come to hold a special, almost sacrosanct place in our public discourse. As I argue in my new book, *Diversity in America: Keeping Government at a Safe Distance*, the social meaning and the importance of diversity have changed. Traditionally, Americans, like all other peoples, feared that too much racial and ethnic diversity could rend the social fabric. But since the civil-rights movement of the 1960s, including the 1965 immigration-law reform, diversity has become an affirmative ideal, with the government using the law to protect and even to promote it. Affirmative action—not just in higher-education admissions but in government contracting, licensing, and public and private employment—is only the most obvious example. Consider several others. Immigration law now distributes 50,000 permanent visas a year through a "diversity lottery" to immigrants whose only special claim is that they come from underrepresented countries. Elementary- and secondary-school systems spend billions of dollars annually for bilingual education designed, in part, to maintain diverse cultural patterns. Judicial decrees mandate ethnic and racial diversity in public-housing programs and ethnic and racial gerrymandering of legislative districts.

The problems of legislating diversity

Ethnic and racial diversity that springs from authentic, spontaneous, voluntary social interactions can have great social value, which is why so many Americans favor it. But when the law tries to mandate diversity, it takes on a difficult task for which it is poorly suited. For example, the law must first decide what diversity means, how to measure it, which groups produce it, how those groups should be defined, whether to subsidize it, and how to enforce it. Governmental decisions like those, instead of increasing diversity's social prestige, may devalue it by rendering it artificial and illegitimate. As each of the examples that I've mentioned demonstrates, such decisions also magnify intergroup and intragroup conflicts over the scarce resources and status that law controls and distributes.

> *Since the civil-rights movement of the 1960s . . . diversity has become an affirmative ideal, with the government using the law to protect and even to promote it.*

That leads to the second point that should be considered concerning affirmative action. Even if the court upholds the constitutionality of one or both of Michigan's plans, does that mean that the state should continue to use it or them? In my view, people planning the next generation of college admissions should consider that ethnic and racial preferences, whether diversity-based or not, constitute poor public policy.

In truth, plans like Michigan's are not really about diversity, but are instead crude efforts to remedy the continuing social disadvantages suffered by black people, with certain other favored groups thrown in. I say "crude efforts" because the plans make all members of a group eligible for preference, even if the individual in question is not in fact disadvantaged and does not have views that would diversify the learning process. That is why most Americans, including many minority-group members, think that such preferences violate the principles of merit and equal opportunity, especially in competitive institutions where the admissions criteria focus on academic performance and promise.

Still, many who are uncomfortable with diversity plans also fear that, without preferences, competitive institutions would include few black stu-

dents, a profoundly troubling outcome in a society seeking to erase the ves-
tiges of racism. That "resegregation" scenario explains the support for affirmative action by thoughtful individuals like Orlando Patterson (*The Ordeal
of Integration: Process and Resentment in America's "Racial" Crisis*, Counter-
point Press, 1997), David Hollinger (*Postethnic America: Beyond Multicultur-
alism*, Basic Books, 1995), Nathan Glazer (*Affirmative Discrimination: Ethnic
Inequality and Public Policy*, Basic Books, 1975), and Derek Bok and William
Bowen (*The Shape of the River: Long-Term Consequences of Considering Race in
College and University Admissions*, Princeton University Press, 1998).

---

*When the law tries to mandate diversity, it takes on
a difficult task for which it is poorly suited.*

But how likely is that nightmare scenario? It is impossible to know
precisely, but defenders of plans like Michigan's only confuse the picture
by arguing, simultaneously, that preferences give only a marginal advantage to minority candidates and that resegregation will follow without
those preferences. Which is it? The sad fact is that black applicants to selective colleges have an average SAT deficit of about 200 points relative to
white students and an even larger deficit in grade-point averages, which,
for admissions purposes, is equivalent to 400 points on the SAT. On the
numbers and without preferences, few black applicants would be admitted to the most competitive institutions.

The percent plans

In fact, however, some of the largest state systems—Texas, California, and
Florida—have adapted to a post-affirmative-action world by instituting
so-called percent plans, which guarantee college admission to the top tier
of students graduating from each high school in the state, even though
some are not otherwise academically qualified. Such plans, moreover, depend on the persistence of segregated high schools, which tragically re-
main all too common. Still, the plans have succeeded in preserving and,
in some cases, increasing minority enrollments in state institutions. Elite
private institutions, for their part, seemed determined to find a way to enroll minority students in a post-affirmative-action world. The *New York
Times* recently reported, for example, that the Rice University admissions
office engages in disingenuous wink-and-nod practices designed to cir-
cumvent the legal prohibition in Texas of straightforward racial and ethnic preferences.

In the public-university systems of states without percent plans, ending affirmative action would be likely to change the distribution of minority students among particular campuses. Since the end of affirmative
action in the California system, a smaller percentage of minority students
now enroll at the most-selective institutions like the University of California at Berkeley, while a greater number attend the University of California at Riverside and other less-competitive campuses.

That is not necessarily a bad outcome. For minority students who
have distressingly high dropout rates from college for academic and fi-

nancial reasons, the redistribution may, in fact, turn out to be a blessing in disguise for many of them. Failing at a more prestigious college for which they are not academically or financially prepared is probably more harmful to their life's prospects than succeeding at a lesser institution. So long as the less-selective colleges provide financial and remedial assistance, and the more-competitive ones engage in active outreach and encourage transfers by students who have demonstrated their academic promise, the results may be fairer, cheaper, and better for all concerned than the distribution among campuses produced by affirmative action.

No one can seriously doubt that the root cause of the relative dearth of minority students in the most-competitive institutions is the vastly inferior elementary and secondary education that minority youngsters receive in too many communities. Affirmative action does not remedy that catastrophe. Quite the contrary, it simply creates a cream-skimming, zero-sum competition among institutions for the relatively few academically qualified minority students—while producing frustration and bitterness for the much larger group of beneficiaries who are ill prepared for the top institutions, and for the even larger group whose races are not preferred. In a post-affirmative-action world, institutions might try to work more closely with inner-city school districts to improve them, as a number of colleges and universities are now doing.

Affirmative action is best left to the private sector

Despite my criticisms of affirmative-action plans, however, I believe that the law should allow private institutions to use them under certain conditions—which is my third point. My criticisms, while relevant to plans in all institutions, apply most strongly to public ones—not just because the Constitution directly binds them, but also because of reasons of public policy and morality. When government speaks, it speaks authoritatively for society, and it inevitably coerces those who disagree with it. That is the nature of public law, for better or worse. In speaking authoritatively, even well-intentioned government-sponsored affirmative-action programs communicate some troubling ideas. They signal that our society thinks it is just and wise to group people by race, to treat those groups monolithically, and to allocate precious resources and opportunities accordingly. Such programs also suggest that we hold equal treatment and individual merit as secondary, dispensable ideals, that the preferred groups cannot succeed without special public favors, and that society thinks we can assuage old injustices by creating new ones.

Because I oppose those ideas, I consider even private affirmative-action programs problematic—but less so than government-sponsored programs. Private institutions speak only for themselves, and they do not generally coerce others. One who opposes a voluntary practice can avoid its burdens more easily than one who opposes a mandated one. A liberal society that values autonomy and diversity has a powerful interest in allowing private individuals to pursue their own ideals and to constitute their communities as they wish. For that reason, a private institution that wants to prefer black students over higher-performing white students, perhaps because it values that kind of diversity more and academic credentials less, should be free to do so—even though it could not legally do the reverse and prefer white students over black students. I may view that preference as profoundly misguided, but I cannot say—and the law should not say—that that choice is unacceptable.

In speaking authoritatively, even well-intentioned government-sponsored affirmative-action programs communicate some troubling ideas.

There are other, more practical reasons why voluntary affirmative-action programs are preferable to legally mandated ones. Voluntary plans tend to be less simplistic and easier to correct or abandon than mandated plans. Voluntary sponsors can tailor their plans to specific needs and contexts. For example, they can define the protected groups differently than affirmative-action law now does, not extending, for example, preferences to black students who are immigrants and thus did not endure a history of discrimination here.

But I would permit private ethnic and racial preferences only under two conditions. First, the preferences must not disadvantage vulnerable minority groups, principally black people, who enjoy special protection under the Constitution. Members of the majority who can readily protect their interests through democratic politics do not need the same legal protection. Second, institutions that use such preferences should be required to publicly disclose them. Current law does not mandate that, and many institutions have opted for obfuscation and outright deception rather than candor. One may argue that silence is golden here, that opacity about ethnic and racial preferences minimizes social disputes over abstract, irreconcilable principles and sustains desirable social myths about equal treatment. Although the argument for opacity has force in some contexts, however, it is notably weak as applied to affirmative action. Here, divisions and suspicions already abound, and dissimulation serves only to magnify and multiply them, as people who assume that preferences are more widespread than they actually are stigmatize even those who did not receive them.

Public disclosure of policies is key

Concealment of the truth about preferences inflames social conflicts and injustices. Requiring institutions to disclose their ethnic and racial preferences in advance would impose a salutary discipline on their use by enabling students, alumni, donors, journalists, and others to hold institutions accountable for their policies—punishing or rewarding them, as the case may be, for practicing a form of discrimination that should continue to be socially controversial, whether or not the law permits it.

Nevertheless, even affirmative action that meets those two conditions may be illegal. Title VI of the Civil Rights Act of 1964 subjects private institutions receiving federal funds to most of the same legal constraints on affirmative action that the Constitution imposes on public programs. The Supreme Court's decision in the Michigan cases may thus clarify the legal status of affirmative action in private institutions as well as public ones. If the court either upholds the Michigan plans or limits them in ways that still leave room for certain kinds of preferences—say, by permitting plans that use race only as a tiebreaker or as a smaller plus factor than Michigan uses—even federally funded private plans can, to that extent, adopt them. (I do not consider state law here, which might limit even privately funded institutions, regardless of how the court resolves the Michigan cases.)

In conclusion, educational institutions and policy makers should not look to the Supreme Court for clear answers to a complex policy question like affirmative action. Whatever the outcome of the Michigan cases, we must resolve this question by deciding what kind of society we wish to be and how our admissions practices contribute to reaching that goal.

6

Affirmative Action Hurts White People

Anne Hull

Anne Hull writes for the Washington Post.

By favoring minorities, affirmative action hurts white people such as Jennifer Gratz. This white female applicant from a working-class Michigan family was rejected by the University of Michigan at Ann Arbor's undergraduate program in 1995, despite her good grades and extracurricular activities. Gratz filed a suit against the university, arguing that affirmative action is discriminatory and that her rejection had destroyed her dreams, irrevocably affecting her life and her decisions.

Jennifer Gratz has heard it all. That she's a pawn of the right. That she's hijacked the language of the civil rights era. That her lawsuit against the University of Michigan's affirmative action policy cloaks a deeper agenda about race.

"Totally crazy," says the 25-year-old, shaking her head.

The facts. In 1995, Gratz was a high school student with a 3.8 GPA, the golden face of her yearbook when she applied to the University of Michigan and was rejected. Two years later, she helped lead a class action lawsuit against the university, alleging that the school's admissions policies gave an unfair edge to minority applicants.

With her case now at the Supreme Court,[1] Gratz has become the central figure in a sprawling ideological debate over affirmative action. It is her story that will challenge the fairness of race-conscious admissions programs: Gratz represents the white working-class striver passed over in the name of diversity.

Affirmative action changed my life

"I can't tell you exactly how my life would be different, because I wasn't given the opportunity," says Gratz, who left Michigan two years ago and

1. The Supreme Court ruled in favor of Gratz.

now lives in the ragged hills north of San Diego. She is not the forensic scientist she thought she'd become; she is a software trainer for a vending machine company called SupplyPro. . . .

To some degree, Gratz was snapped into machinery that was churning before she received her rejection letter. The battle began in 1978 when the Supreme Court ruled in *Regents of the University of California v. Bakke* that race could be used as a factor in admitting students but that quotas were forbidden. In 1996, a federal appeals court in Texas barred the consideration of race in admissions and financial aid.

In 1995, events were taking hold in Michigan. A cache of documents forced into public view revealed Michigan's admissions process. The group of lawyers who won the Texas case was looking for another. From this confluence emerged Gratz.

Gratz wasn't an activist or grass-roots warrior. She was a teenager whose rejection by her dream school shook her confidence and sense of fairness. She had spent years polishing her credentials for the University of Michigan, working hard, volunteering, studying, even chairing blood drives. Then the dream was snatched away. A minority student with the same GPA and test scores as Gratz would have likely been accepted under Michigan's policy.

Diversity at Michigan

Michigan acknowledges that it weighs race when considering applicants. To process the more than 25,000 undergraduate applications that flood in each year for the 5,000 coveted spots, the school uses a point system to score each prospective student. Black, Latino and Native American applicants are awarded extra points because they belong to groups the university says are underrepresented on campus. In the 2002 class, blacks made up almost 9 percent of Michigan's freshman class, Latinos 6 percent and Native Americans almost 2 percent.

"We want to have a class that thinks about issues from different backgrounds," says Mary Sue Coleman, the university's president.

The notion galls Gratz. Atmospheres can't be "engineered," she says. Points for being a minority?

"That would be like me deciding, 'Hey, I want to feed the hungry but I don't have any means to do that, so I'm going to go rob a grocery store,'" she says. "It's still illegal, even though my intentions are good."

The University of Michigan is one of the most idyllic campuses in America. On fall Saturdays, when 107,000 fans jam into Michigan Stadium and shatter NCAA attendance records, a sonic halo lifts over Ann Arbor. The splendor is secondary to academics: Michigan is one of two public institutions consistently ranked among the nation's top 10 universities.

Gratz's story

Gratz grew up 45 minutes away in Southgate, a working-class suburb of Detroit where many in her neighborhood pulled shift work at the auto assembly plants. Her dad was a police sergeant who worked $10-an-hour moonlighting jobs as a security guard; her mom was a secretary. Neither parent finished college. On Saturday afternoons in the Gratz house, Michigan football ruled the TV. Gratz attended St. Pius Catholic School through the eighth grade and then set her sights on studying forensic medicine at Michigan.

At Southgate Anderson High, she did it all: student government, National Honor Society, science club, spirit club, cheerleader. . . .

"Jennifer did everything we asked her to do, and more," says a former assistant principal, Ron Dittmer. "I wouldn't ask any more of my own daughter."

Gratz represents the white working-class striver passed over in the name of diversity.

Gratz was so confident that she'd make the cut at Michigan that she applied to no other colleges. The wait-list letter was the first bad sign. Then in April of her senior year, after weeks of running home from school to check the mail, came the thin letter of rejection. Through her tears, Gratz uttered her now-famous rejoinder: "Dad, can we sue?"

It was an odd reaction for a 17-year-old. But Gratz said she suspected something amiss, if not precisely that she'd been passed over because she was white. "Everyone knew bits and pieces," she says, about the premium Michigan placed on diversity. Gratz was in a state of shock. She was so embarrassed by the rejection that she told no one, not even her boyfriend of three years. She hurriedly applied to the University of Notre Dame but didn't get in. She was accepted into the honors program at the University of Michigan's campus in Dearborn. . . .

"You've got four or five buildings where you take your classes," Gratz says [of Dearborn], with none of the luminosity she reserves to describe Ann Arbor. "No dorms, the U-Mall with 40 or 50 tables where you could sit around waiting for your next class to start. It wasn't college.". . .

Around the same time, a University of Michigan philosophy professor named Carl Cohen read in the *Journal of Blacks in Higher Education* that acceptance rates for blacks at top-tier universities were higher than for whites. Suspicious of his own university's admissions system, Cohen filed a Freedom of Information Act request.

The documents showed that Michigan used a grid to evaluate applicants, in part based on race. The grid launched everything: Cohen's testimony before the Michigan legislature sparked four Republican lawmakers to take up the cause.

A plaintiff is born

One of the politicians was then–state Rep. Deborah Whyman, who called the Center for Individual Rights, a conservative Washington law firm that was hot off its 1996 victory in the Texas affirmative action case.

"We laid out a game plan," says Whyman. "When it came down to finding plaintiffs, I did it." She did talk radio shows and gave news interviews about a possible lawsuit against Michigan.

Gratz's parents saw a newspaper article and clipped it for their daughter, who was working at a summer cheerleading camp but still living at home. Immediately, Gratz knew she wanted to be part of some effort against Michigan. She pictured herself stuffing envelopes. She called Whyman's office and gave her vital statistics: her high school GPA, test scores and extracurricular activities.

Gratz wasn't an activist or grass-roots warrior. She was a teenager whose rejection by her dream school shook her confidence and sense of fairness.

Whyman says she forwarded 200 names to CIR; the law firm's Curt Levey says that only "six or seven" were ever seriously considered. One was Gratz, who met with CIR attorneys at a Courtyard Marriott near the Detroit airport. A plaintiff was born.

The lawsuit was filed in October 1997 on behalf of Gratz and Patrick Hamacher, another student wait-listed from Michigan's undergraduate program. A separate lawsuit was filed against the University of Michigan Law School. Oral arguments in both cases are scheduled for April 1 [2003] before the Supreme Court.

Gratz absorbed most of the heat. Walking out of the courthouse after her case had been sent to the U.S. Court of Appeals for the 6th Circuit, a protester screamed at Gratz, "racist bitch!"

"I'm exactly the opposite," she would later say. "I'm standing up and saying people should not be treated differently because of their skin color."

After Cohen's documents were made public, Michigan changed its admissions process, replacing the grid with the point system that is being challenged. On this "Selection Index Worksheet," a perfect GPA is worth 80 points. Having a parent who attended Michigan is worth up to four points. Scholarship athletes are awarded 20 points. A perfect SAT score brings 12 points and an excellent essay gets one point. Being an under-represented minority brings 20 points.

"To assume a minority can't go to the University of Michigan without that 20 points is crazy," says Gratz. "There are plenty of kids who could stand on their own."

Gratz has been confronted with every angle of the argument. Aren't legacy points also a form of preference? "Four points," she says, not 20. Besides, minorities can also be legacies.

In a classroom setting, could a black student's viewpoints enrich a discussion about racial profiling? "Everyone in the country views racial profiling as wrong," Gratz says. "That's exactly what the University of Michigan is doing: racial profiling. There are race-neutral ways to run an admissions process."

What about affirmative action acting as a remedy for society's past discriminatory practices? Her lawyer won't allow her to answer. "That's a policy question," says Levey.

As for her own life, Gratz says she decided not to transfer to Ann Arbor after her sophomore year at Dearborn; too many of her core courses wouldn't have carried over. She received her math degree in 1999. She took a job with a credit union in Michigan, continuing to live at home. She then switched to a Los Angeles–based company, which brought her to California. . . .

Gratz says she was sidetracked by a system that works against whites, but she has made the best of her life. "I'm not an angry or bitter person," she says, gently picking up one of her cats, Bandit. . . .

Asked if it's hard to think about minority students who walk the grounds of the Ann Arbor campus, Gratz says with the slightest bit of edge, "They've been given an opportunity to go to an excellent school. Good for them."

7

The Claim That Affirmative Action Hurts White People Is a Myth

Goodwin Liu

Goodwin Liu, an attorney living in Washington, D.C., was a Supreme Court law clerk for the 2000/2001 year.

Many white people, particularly applicants who have been rejected from selective educational institutions, feel that affirmative action hurts whites. They feel discriminated against. But despite their perception, statistics clearly show that affirmative action hardly reduces their chance of admission at all. This is because although minorities may be admitted to selective institutions at higher rates, the small numbers of minorities in real terms as compared with the still overwhelmingly white pool of applicants means that affirmative action does not hurt the majority in any statistically significant way. Affirmative action can thus have a profound impact on a few minority individuals while barely affecting the majority.

With the arrival of spring, thousands of high school and college seniors have been anxiously checking the mail for word from the nation's most prestigious universities. Although some envelopes are thick with good news, most are thin and disappointing. For many white applicants, the disappointment will become bitterness if they suspect the reason for their rejection was affirmative action. But such suspicions, in all likelihood, are misplaced.

Affirmative action is widely thought to be unfair because it benefits minority applicants at the expense of more deserving whites. Yet this perception tends to inflate the cost beyond its real proportions. While it is true that affirmative action gives minority applicants a significant boost in selective admissions, it is not true that most white applicants would fare better if elite schools eliminated the practice. Understanding why is crucial to separating fact from fiction in the national debate over affirmative action.

White anger at affirmative action

Any day now, a federal appeals court in Cincinnati will issue a decision in a major test lawsuit challenging the use of race as a factor in selective admissions. In that case, the University of Michigan denied admission in 1995 to a white undergraduate applicant named Jennifer Gratz. Charging reverse discrimination, Gratz said, "I knew of people accepted to Ann Arbor who were less qualified, and my first reaction when I was rejected was, 'Let's sue.'" The Michigan case will likely end up at the Supreme Court.[1] If it does, Gratz will try to follow in the footsteps of Allan Bakke, a rejected white applicant who won admission in 1978 to the University of California at Davis's medical school after convincing the high court that the school's policy of reserving 16 of 100 seats each year for minority students was unconstitutional. For many Americans, the success of Bakke's lawsuit has long highlighted what is unfair about affirmative action: Giving minority applicants a significant advantage causes deserving white applicants to lose out. But to draw such an inference in Bakke's case—or in the case of the vast majority of rejected white applicants—is to indulge in what I call "the causation fallacy."

The 1978 *Bakke* case

There's no doubt, based on test scores and grades, that Bakke was a highly qualified applicant. Justice Lewis Powell, who authored the decisive opinion in the case, observed that Bakke's Medical College Admission Test (MCAT) scores placed him in the top tier of test-takers, whereas the average scores of the quota beneficiaries in 1974 placed them in the bottom third. Likewise, his science grade point average was 3.44 on a 4.0 scale, compared with a 2.42 average for the special admittees, and his overall GPA was similarly superior. Given these numbers, the only reason for Bakke's rejection was the school's need to make room for less qualified minority applicants, right?

Affirmative action is widely thought to be unfair because it benefits minority applicants at the expense of more deserving whites.

Wrong. Although Justice Powell pointed out that minority applicants were admitted with grades and test scores much lower than Bakke's, he did not discuss what I found to be the most striking data that appeared in his opinion: Bakke's grades and scores were significantly higher than the average for the regular admittees. In other words, his academic qualifications were better than those of the majority of applicants admitted outside the racial quota. So why didn't he earn one of the 84 regular places?

1. The Supreme Court ruled in favor of Gratz.

It is clear that the medical school admitted students not only on the basis of grades and test scores, but on other factors relevant to the study and practice of medicine, such as compassion, communication skills and commitment to research. Justice Powell's opinion does not tell us exactly what qualities the regular admittees had that Bakke lacked. But it notes that the head of the admissions committee, who interviewed Bakke, found him "rather limited in his approach" to medical problems and thought he had "very definite opinions which were based more on his personal viewpoints than upon a study of the total problem."

Whatever Bakke's weaknesses were, there were several reasons, apart from affirmative action, that might have led the medical school to reject his application. Grades and test scores do not tell us the whole story.

Eliminating racial preferences would have increased the likelihood of admission for white undergraduate applicants from 25 percent to only 26.5 percent.

Of course, affirmative action did lower Bakke's chance of admission. But by how much? One way to answer this question is to compare Bakke's chance of admission had he competed for all 100 seats in the class with his chance of admission competing for the 84 seats outside of the racial quota. To simplify, let's assume none of the special applicants would have been admitted ahead of any regular candidate.

In 1974, Bakke was one of 3,109 regular applicants to the medical school. With the racial quota, the average likelihood of admission for regular applicants was 2.7 percent (84 divided by 3,109). With no racial quota, the average likelihood of admission would have been 3.2 percent (100 divided by 3,109). So the quota increased the average likelihood of rejection from 96.8 percent to 97.3 percent.

To be sure, Bakke was not an average applicant. Only one-sixth of regular applicants (roughly 520) received an interview. But even among these highly qualified applicants, eliminating the racial quota would have increased the average rate of admission from 16 percent (84 divided by 520) to only 19 percent (100 divided by 520). Certainly a few more regular applicants would have been admitted were it not for affirmative action. But Bakke, upon receiving his rejection letter, had no reason to believe he would have been among the lucky few.

In fact, Bakke applied in both 1973 and 1974 and, according to evidence in the lawsuit, he did not even make the waiting list in either year.

The statistical pattern in Bakke's case is not an anomaly. It occurs in any selection process in which the applicants who do not benefit from affirmative action greatly outnumber those who do.

Recent research confirms this point. Using 1989 data from a representative sample of selective schools, former university presidents William Bowen and Derek Bok showed in their 1998 book, *The Shape of the River*, that eliminating racial preferences would have increased the likelihood of admission for white undergraduate applicants from 25 percent to only 26.5 percent.

Affirmative action does not statistically hurt majority applicants

The Mellon Foundation, which sponsored the study, provided me with additional data to calculate admission rates by SAT score. If the schools in the Bowen/Bok sample had admitted applicants with similar SAT scores at the same rate regardless of race, the chance of admission for white applicants would have increased by one percentage point or less at scores 1300 and above, by three to four percentage points at scores from 1150 to 1299, and by four to seven percentage points at scores below 1150.

It is true that black applicants were admitted at much higher rates than white applicants with similar grades and test scores. But that fact does not prove that affirmative action imposes a substantial disadvantage on white applicants. The extent of the disadvantage depends on the number of blacks and whites in the applicant pool. Because the number of black applicants to selective institutions is relatively small, admitting them at higher rates does not significantly lower the chance of admission for the average individual in the relatively large sea of white applicants.

In the Bowen/Bok study, for example, 60 percent of black applicants scoring 1200–1249 on the SAT were admitted, compared with 19 percent of whites. In the 1250–1299 range, 74 percent of blacks were admitted, compared with 23 percent of whites. These data indicate—more so than proponents of affirmative action typically acknowledge—that racial preferences give minority applicants a substantial advantage. But eliminating affirmative action would have increased the admission rate for whites from 19 percent to only 21 percent in the 1200–1249 range, and from 23 percent to only 24 percent in the 1250–1299 range.

In selective admissions, the competition is so intense that even without affirmative action, the overwhelming majority of rejected white applicants still wouldn't get in.

These figures show that rejected white applicants have every reason not to blame their misfortune on affirmative action. In selective admissions, the competition is so intense that even without affirmative action, the overwhelming majority of rejected white applicants still wouldn't get in.

There are many types of preferences

Still, isn't it true that minority applicants are admitted at rates up to three times higher than white applicants with similar SAT scores? Isn't that unfair?

To answer that question, it's important to observe that racial preferences are not the only preferences that cause different groups of applicants with similar test scores to be admitted at different rates. Geographic, athletic and alumni preferences also weigh heavily, to the detriment of applicants such as Jennifer Gratz at Michigan. Gratz hailed from a Detroit suburb, not from a rural area or the inner city. She was not a star athlete. And her working-class parents were high school graduates, not University of Michigan alumni.

Yet preferences for athletes, though occasionally criticized, have never galvanized the kind of outrage often directed at affirmative action. Similarly, there is no organized legal campaign against geographic preferences, even though where one grows up is as much an accident of circumstance as one's skin color. And neither Gratz nor her lawyers at the Washington-based Center for Individual Rights have publicly denounced alumni preferences, much less launched a moral crusade against them.

Such preferences reflect institutional interests that are unrelated to an applicant's grades or test scores. But the same is true of affirmative action when it is used to enhance educational diversity. The question, then, is not whether unequal treatment is unfair as a general rule, but whether unequal treatment based on race should be singled out for special condemnation.

As the Supreme Court said in 1954, unequal treatment based on race can inflict on members of a disfavored race "a feeling of inferiority as to their status in the community that may affect their hearts and minds in a way unlikely ever to be undone." But social stigma is not the complaint pressed by white applicants such as Bakke or Gratz. Despite 30 years of affirmative action, white students continue to dominate most of the nation's best colleges and all of the top law and medical schools. Against this backdrop, not even the most ardent foe of affirmative action would say that it stamps white applicants with a badge of racial inferiority. Indeed, just as athletic and geographic preferences do not denigrate applicants who are uncoordinated or suburban, affirmative action is not a policy of racial prejudice.

For white applicants, the unfairness of affirmative action lies not in its potential to displace or stigmatize, but in its potential to stereotype. Minority applicants are not the only ones who contribute to educational diversity. Were a school to use race as its sole "plus" factor in admissions, then white applicants could legitimately complain that the school failed to take into account non-racial attributes essential to genuine educational diversity.

Putting the complaint in these terms is an important first step toward rethinking the conventional view that a race-conscious admissions policy pits whites against minorities in a zero-sum game. Instead of attacking affirmative action, white applicants such as Jennifer Gratz might do better to urge top schools committed to educational diversity to place a higher premium on first-generation college attendance or growing up in a blue-collar home. Ironically, the stories of affirmative action's "victims" could spur America's colleges to further widen the elite circles of educational opportunity. And that would be a result students of any color could applaud.

8

Affirmative Action Is Necessary in Higher Education

Patricia Gurin, Eric L. Dey,
Sylvia Hurtado, and Gerald Gurin

Patricia Gurin is chair of the department of psychology at the University of Michigan. Eric L. Dey is executive associate dean and an associate professor at the University of Michigan school of education. Sylvia Hurtado is associate professor and director of the Center for the Study of Higher and Postsecondary Education at the University of Michigan. Gerald Gurin is a professor and research scientist emeritus at the University of Michigan.

Creating ethnically and racially diverse student bodies through affirmative action policies improves higher education. Students who attend colleges where the ethnic and racial composition is different from that of their hometowns are more inclined to think critically than are students who go to schools where the student body is racially and ethnically similar to that of their hometowns. Such cognitive growth helps students interact with and learn from people different from themselves, which is essential for navigating an increasingly heterogeneous and complex society.

E ducators in U.S. higher education have long argued that affirmative action policies are justified because they ensure the creation of the racially and ethnically diverse student bodies essential to providing the best possible educational environment for students, white and minority alike. Yet until recently these arguments have lacked empirical evidence and a strong theoretical rationale to support the link between diversity and educational outcomes. As Jonathan Alger, former counsel for the American Association of University Professors, argues: "The unfinished homework in the affirmative action debate concerns the development of an articulated vision—supported by a strong evidentiary basis—of the educational benefits of racial diversity in higher education." This suggests not only that educators must clarify the conceptual link between diversity and learning in educational practice, but also that educational researchers play a key role in providing evidence on whether diversity contributes to achieving the central goals of higher education. The purpose of this article is both to provide a theory of how diversity can be linked to educational outcomes in higher education and to test this theory using national data and data from students at the University of Michigan— an institution that has faced affirmative action legal challenges. . . .

Diversity exposure

It is important to explain how higher education might expose students to racial and ethnic diversity, since they may experience it in several ways. First, students attend colleges with different levels of racial/ethnic diversity in their student bodies. This has been termed *structural diversity*, or the numerical representation of diverse groups. Although structural diversity increases the probability that students will encounter others of diverse backgrounds, given the U.S. history of race relations, simply attending an ethnically diverse college does not guarantee that students will have the meaningful intergroup interactions that social psychologist Gordon Allport suggested in his classic book, *The Nature of Prejudice*, are important for the reduction of racial prejudice. For this reason, a second definition of racial/ethnic diversity is important, one that involves both the *frequency* and the *quality* of intergroup interaction as keys to meaningful diversity experiences during college, or what we term *informal interaction diversity*. Although these informal interactions with racially diverse peers can occur in many campus contexts, the majority of them occur outside of the classroom. Such interactions may include informal discussions, daily interactions in residence halls, campus events, and social activities. Finally, a third form of diversity experience includes learning about diverse people (content knowledge) and gaining experience with diverse peers in the classroom, or what we term *classroom diversity*. We contend that the impact of racial/ethnic diversity on educational outcomes comes primarily from engagement with diverse peers in the informal campus environment and in college classrooms. Structural diversity is a necessary but insufficient condition for maximal educational benefits; therefore, the theory that guides our study is based on students' actual engagement with diverse peers.

Recent reviews of educational research, as well as summaries of new studies, present an emerging body of scholarship that speaks directly to the benefits of a racially/ethnically diverse postsecondary educational experience. The evidence for the diversity rationale for affirmative action has come from four approaches to research:

1. students' subjective assessments of the benefits they receive from interacting with diverse peers

2. faculty assessments about the impact of diversity on student learning or on other outcomes related to the missions of their universities

3. analyses of monetary and nonmonetary returns to students and the larger community in terms of graduation rates, attainment of advanced and professional degrees that prepare students to become leaders

in underserved communities, personal income or other postcollege attainment that results from attending highly selective institutions where affirmative action is critical to achieving diversity

4. analyses tying diversity experience during the college years to a wide variety of educational outcomes

It is important to note that, across these different approaches and different samples of students and faculty, researchers have found similar results showing that a wide variety of individual, institutional, and societal benefits are linked with diversity experiences.

The research reported here is an example of the fourth approach in which we compare how different types of diversity experiences are associated with differences in educational outcomes among students from different racial and ethnic backgrounds. We first present the theoretical foundation for the educational value of racial/ethnic diversity, and then we examine the effects of two kinds of diversity experiences—diversity in the formal classroom and in the informal campus environment—on different educational outcomes.

Racial and ethnic diversity may promote a broad range of educational outcomes, but we focus on two general categories. Learning outcomes include active thinking skills, intellectual engagement and motivation, and a variety of academic skills. Democracy outcomes include perspective-taking, citizenship engagement, racial and cultural understanding, and judgment of the compatibility among different groups in a democracy. The impact of diversity on learning and democracy outcomes is believed to be especially important during the college years because students are at a critical developmental stage, which takes place in institutions explicitly constituted to promote late adolescent development.

Intellectual experimentation

In essays that profoundly affected our understanding of social development, psychologist Erik Erikson introduced the concept of identity and argued that late adolescence and early adulthood are the unique times when a sense of personal and social identity is formed. Identity involves two important elements: a persistent sameness within oneself and a persistent sharing with others. Erikson theorized that identity develops best when young people are given a psychosocial moratorium—a time and a place in which they can experiment with different social roles before making permanent commitments to an occupation, to intimate relationships, to social and political groups and ideas, and to a philosophy of life. We argue that such a moratorium should ideally involve a confrontation with diversity and complexity, lest young people passively make commitments based on their past experiences, rather than actively think and make decisions informed by new and more complex perspectives and relationships.

Institutions of higher education can provide an opportunity for such a psychosocial moratorium, thus supporting young adults through this identity development stage. Residential colleges and universities provide many students with an opportunity to experiment with new ideas, new relationships, and new roles. Peer influences play a normative role in this development, and students are able to explore options and possibilities before making permanent adult commitments. Yet not all institutions of higher education serve this developmental function equally well. Higher education is especially influential when its social milieu is different from students' home and community background and when it is diverse and complex enough to encourage intellectual experimentation and recognition of varied future possibilities. We maintain that attending college in one's home environment or replicating the home community's social life and expectations in a homogeneous college that is simply an extension of the home community impedes the personal struggle and conscious thought that are so important for identity development.

Affirmative action policies . . . ensure the creation of the racially and ethnically diverse student bodies essential to providing the best possible [education].

Sociologist Theodore Newcomb's classic study of students at Bennington College supported Erikson's assertion that late adolescence is a time to determine one's relationship to the sociopolitical world and affirmed the developmental impact of the college experience. Newcomb's study demonstrated that political and social attitudes—what Erikson would call one aspect of social identity—are quite malleable in late adolescence and that change occurred particularly in those students to whom Bennington presented new and different ideas and attitudes. Peer influence was critical in shaping the attitudinal changes that Newcomb documented. Follow-ups with these students showed that the attitudes formed during the college experience were quite stable, even twenty-five and fifty years later.

Developmental theorists emphasize that discontinuity and discrepancy spur cognitive growth. Jean Piaget termed this process *disequilibrium.* Drawing on these theories, psychologist Diane Ruble offers a model that ties developmental change to life transitions such as going to college. Transitions are significant because they present new situations about which individuals know little and in which they will experience uncertainty. The early phase of a transition, what Ruble calls construction, is especially important, since people have to seek information in order to make sense of the new situation. Under these conditions individuals are likely to undergo cognitive growth unless they are able to retreat to a familiar world. Ruble's model gives special importance to the first year of college, since it is during this time that classroom and social relationships discrepant from students' home environments become especially important in fostering cognitive growth.

Writing long before the controversies about diversity and affirmative action became politically important or were studied academically, Erikson, Newcomb, and Piaget were not making an explicit case for racial/ethnic diversity. Nonetheless, their arguments about the significance of discontinuity and the power of a late adolescence/early adulthood moratorium provide a strong theoretical rationale for the importance of bringing students from varied backgrounds together to create a diverse and complex learning environment.

Campus environments and policies that foster interaction among diverse students are discontinuous from the home environments of many

American students. Because of the racial separation that persists in this country, most students have lived in segregated communities before coming to college. The work of Gary Orfield and associates documents a deepening segregation in U.S. public schools. This segregated precollege educational background means that many students, white and minority alike, enter college without experience with diverse peers. Colleges that diversify their student bodies and institute policies that foster genuine interaction across race and ethnicity provide the first opportunity for many students to learn from peers with different cultures, values, and experiences. Genuine interaction goes far beyond mere contact and includes learning about difference in background, experience, and perspectives, as well as getting to know one another individually in an intimate enough way to discern common goals and personal qualities. In this kind of interaction—in and out of the classroom—diverse peers will learn from each other. This can be viewed as extending the traditional conception of a liberal education as one "intended to break down the narrow certainties and provincial vision with which we are born," [according to the Association of American Colleges and Universities]. . . .

Designing curricula for active thinking

We might expect that a curriculum that deals explicitly with social and cultural diversity and a learning environment in which diverse students interact frequently with one another would affect the content of what is learned. However, based on the recent social psychological research that we discuss below, we consider the less obvious notion that features of the learning environment affect students' modes of thought. In this study we hypothesize that a curriculum that exposes students to knowledge about race and ethnicity acquired through the curriculum and classroom environment and to interactions with peers from diverse racial and ethnic backgrounds in the informal college environment will foster a learning environment that supports active thinking and intellectual engagement.

Higher education is especially influential when its social milieu is . . . diverse . . . enough to encourage intellectual experimentation.

Research in social psychology over the past twenty years has shown that active engagement in learning and thinking cannot be assumed. This research confirms that much apparent thinking and thoughtful action are actually automatic, or what psychologist Ellen Langer calls mindless. To some extent, mindlessness is the result of previous learning that has become so routine that thinking is unnecessary. Instead, scripts or schemas that are activated and operate automatically guide these learned routines. Some argue that mindlessness is necessary because there are too many stimuli in the world to which to pay attention. It is more efficient for us to select only a few stimuli or, better still, to go on automatic pilot—to be what some people call cognitive misers.

Psychologist John Bargh reviews both historical and recent research evidence showing that automatic psychological processes play a pervasive role in all aspects of everyday thinking. He concludes that automatic thinking is evident not only in perceptual processes (such as categorization) and in the execution of perceptional and motor skills (such as driving and typing), but that it is also pervasive in evaluation, emotional reactions, determination of goals, and social behavior itself. Bargh uses the term *preconscious* to describe processes that act as mental servants to take over from conscious, effortful thinking. One of our tasks as educators is to interrupt these automatic processes and facilitate active thinking in our students.

Diverse peers will learn from each other.

In one early study indicating the pervasiveness of automatic thinking, Langer described the many positive psychological benefits that people derive from using active, effortful, conscious modes of thought. She also argued that such thinking helps people develop new ideas and ways of processing information that may have been available to them but were simply not often used. In several experimental studies, she showed that such thinking increases alertness and greater mental activity, which fosters better learning and supports the developmental goals of higher education.

What are the conditions that encourage effortful, mindful, and conscious modes of thought? Langer contends that people will engage in such modes of thought when they encounter a situation for which they have no script or when the environment demands more than their current scripts provide, such as an encounter discrepant with their past experience. These conditions are similar to what sociologist Rose Coser calls complex social structures—situations where we encounter people who are unfamiliar to us, when these people challenge us to think or act in new ways, when people and relationships change and thus produce unpredictability, and when people we encounter hold different expectations of us. Coser shows that people who function within complex social structures develop a clearer and stronger sense of individuality and a deeper understanding of the social world.

Personal development

The specific environmental features that Langer and Coser suggest will promote mental activity are compatible with cognitive-developmental theories. In general, those theories posit that cognitive growth is fostered by discontinuity and discrepancy (as in Piaget's notion of disequilibrium). To learn or grow cognitively, individuals need to recognize cognitive conflicts or contradictions, situations that, as psychologist Diane Ruble argues, then lead to a state of uncertainty, instability, and possibly anxiety. Ruble states:

> Such a state may occur for a number of reasons. . . . It may be generated either internally via the recognition of incompatible cognitions or externally during social interaction. The latter is particularly relevant to many types of life transitions, because such transitions are likely to alter the prob-

ability of encountering people whose viewpoints differ from one's own.

Racial and ethnic diversity in the student body and university efforts to foster opportunities for diverse students to interact and learn from each other in and out of the classroom offer college students who have grown up in the racially segregated United States the very features that these theories suggest will foster active thinking and personal development. These features include:

• novelty and unfamiliarity that occurs upon the transition to college

• opportunities to identify discrepancies between students with distinct pre-college social experiences

A white student, evaluating a course on intergroup relations that one of the authors taught at the University of Michigan, conveys the importance of these facets of diversity:

> I come from a town in Michigan where everyone was white, middle-class and generally pretty closed-down to the rest of the world, although we didn't think so. It never touched us, so I never questioned the fact that we were "normal" and everyone else was "different." Listening to other students in the class, especially the African American students from Detroit and other urban areas just blew me away. We only live a few hours away and yet we live in completely separate worlds. Even more shocking was the fact that they knew about "my world" and I knew nothing about theirs. Nor did I think that this was even a problem at first. I realize now that many people like me can go through life and not have to see another point of view, that somehow we are protected from it. The beginning for me was when I realized that not everyone shares the same views as I, and that our different experiences have a lot to do with that.

One of our primary goals was to discover whether such encounters with diversity contribute to learning outcomes, not only among students at the University of Michigan but also among those attending a variety of four-year institutions across the country. A second key goal was to understand the extent to which these same diversity experiences contribute to the development of the skills and dispositions that students will need to be leaders in a pluralistic democracy.

Good for democracy

From the time the founding fathers debated what form U.S. democracy should take—representational or directly participatory—education has been seen as the key to achieving an informed citizenry. In the compromise they reached involving both representation and broad participation, education was the mechanism that was to make broad participation possible. Benjamin Barber argues that it was [Thomas] Jefferson, certainly no advocate of diversity, who most forcefully argued that broad civic participation required education: "It remained clear to Jefferson to the end of his life that a theory of democracy that is rooted in active participation and continuing consent by each generation of citizens demands a civic pedagogy rooted in the obligation to educate all who would be citizens." To be sure, Jefferson was talking about education for those he defined as the body of citizens and not for the many who were not citizens at that time.

If education is the very foundation of democracy, how do experiences with racial/ethnic diversity affect the process of learning to become citizens? We contend that students educated in diverse institutions will be more motivated and better able to participate in an increasingly heterogeneous and complex society. In *Democratic Education in an Age of Difference*, Richard Guarasci and Grant Cornwell concur, claiming that "community and democratic citizenship are strengthened when undergraduates understand and experience social connections with those outside of their often parochial 'autobiographies,' and when they experience the way their lives are necessarily shaped by others."

Students educated in diverse institutions will be more motivated and better able to participate in an increasingly . . . complex society.

However, the compatibility of diversity and democracy is not self-evident. Current critics of multicultural education worry that identities based on race, ethnicity, gender, class, and other categorizations are inimical to the unity needed for democracy. Yet the tension between unity and diversity, however politically charged, is not new in the United States.

In *Fear of Diversity*, Arlene Saxonhouse describes how the pre-Socratic playwrights as well as Plato and Aristotle dealt with the fear that "differences bring on chaos and thus demand that the world be put into an orderly pattern." While Plato envisioned a city in which unity and harmony would be based on the shared characteristics of a homogeneous citizenry, Aristotle recognized the value of heterogeneity and welcomed the diverse. Saxonhouse writes: "Aristotle embraces diversity as the others had not. . . . The typologies that fill almost every page of Aristotle's *Politics* show him uniting and separating, finding underlying unity and significant differences." Aristotle advanced a political theory in which unity could be achieved through differences and contended that democracy based on such a unity would be more likely to thrive than one based on homogeneity. What makes democracy work, according to Aristotle, is equality among citizens (admittedly, in his time only free men, not women or slaves) who hold diverse perspectives and whose relationships are governed by freedom and rules of civil discourse. It is a multiplicity of perspectives and discourses in response to the inevitable conflicts that arise when citizens have differing points of view, not unanimity, that help democracy thrive.

A complex, heterogeneous society

Diversity, plurality, equality, and freedom are also implied in Piaget's theory of intellectual and moral development. He argues that children and adolescents can best develop a capacity to understand the ideas and feelings of others—what he calls perspective-taking—and move to a more advanced stage of moral reasoning when they interact with peers who have different points of view. Both differing perspectives and equality in relationships are important for intellectual and moral development. In a homogeneous environment in which young people are not forced to confront the relativity or limitations of their point of view, they are likely to conform to a single perspective defined by an authority. In a hierarchical environment in which young people are not obliged to discuss and argue with others on an equal basis, they are not likely to do the cognitive and emotional work that is required to understand how other people think and feel. These cognitive and emotional processes promote the moral development needed to make a pluralistic democracy work.

In the United States, however, common conceptions of democracy do not treat difference as being compatible with unity. In general, popular understandings of democracy and citizenship take one of two forms: 1) a liberal individualist conception in which citizens participate by voting for public servants to represent them and by other individual acts, and 2) a direct participatory conception in which people from similar backgrounds who are familiar with each other come together to debate the common good, as in the New England town meeting. Both of these conceptions privilege individuals and similarities rather than groups and differences.

The increasingly heterogeneous U.S. population challenges these popular conceptions of democracy. Consequently, we are now facing cultural, academic, and political debates over the extent to which American democracy can survive increasing heterogeneity and group-based social and political claims. Yet, it is clear that an ethnic hierarchy or one-way assimilation, both of which call for muting differences and cultural identities, is much less likely to prevail than in the past.

The theories of Aristotle and Piaget both suggest that difference and democracy can be compatible. The conditions deemed important for this compatibility include the presence of diverse others and diverse perspectives, equality among peers, and discussion according to rules of civil discourse. We hypothesize that these conditions foster the orientations that students will need to be citizens and leaders in the postcollege world: perspective-taking, mutuality and reciprocity, acceptance of conflict as a normal part of life, capacity to perceive differences and commonalties both within and between social groups, interest in the wider social world, and citizen participation.

9

Affirmative Action Has No Place in Higher Education

Richard F. Tomasson

The late Richard F. Tomasson was chairman of the sociology department at the University of New Mexico.

There should be no affirmative action in any universities. Any system of preferences is unjust, whether it is affirmative action, or even worse, the favoritism of so-called "legacy" admissions (when colleges give preference to applicants whose parent or grandparent attended that college). Moreover, admissions decisions should also not be based on such things as character and extracurricular activities or personal achievements: Grades and test scores should be the *sole* criterion for admission to the nation's most selective institutions. There are sufficient numbers of colleges in the United States for all students to attend, which means that if affirmative action were abolished and minority enrollment at elite institutions dropped, minorities could attend the slightly less-competitive institutions where they would still receive a good education.

Affirmative action for designated race and ethnic categories in higher education is, at worst, patronizing, corrupting, and eventually demoralizing to its intended beneficiaries; at best, quite unnecessary in a country oversupplied with colleges and universities.

Actually, preferential undergraduate admissions has relevance for only a tiny, but very significant, proportion of colleges and universities, those that are able to be selective. Fewer than 5 percent of freshmen are enrolled in the twenty-five "top" universities and the twenty-five "top" small colleges. The great majority enroll in institutions that require little more than graduating from high school along with some mild provisions regarding grades or test scores. Some state schools have no admission requirements at all beyond high school graduation; in a few states, law mandates admission to any graduate of a high school in the state. Community colleges admit anyone.

But to elite colleges and universities affirmative action is an obsessive concern. The most touted public reason is to achieve a diverse student body. The old reason, to compensate for past hurtful discrimination, has faded away as the clients of affirmative action have expanded beyond blacks to include other groups for whom the claim of past discrimination is less compelling, or not compelling at all. (Interestingly and revealingly, there is a virtual absence of gender-based affirmative action in higher education.)

All preferences are wrong

There is another sort of preference, much less publicly celebrated by universities than that of achieving ethnic diversity. It is an affirmative action for the privileged. And it is used to justify race and ethnic preferences. If a college gives special treatment to the offspring of alumni, so goes the argument, is it not equally just to give similar treatment to minority applicants? Can one accept the former sort of preference and not the latter? Isn't there a *quid pro quid* here? If being an alumnus offspring is treated as a plus when applying to Dartmouth, fairness would seem to insist that being a minority person should also be treated as a plus. Justice Lewis Powell argued just this in his famous *Bakke* opinion of 1978, but, as John Jeffries, Jr., has written in his biography of the justice, he intended it to be only a temporary measure, maybe to last a decade. What the justice feared was that special admissions programs like those at Davis "would become entrenched bureaucracies, and minorities would come to regard them as perpetual entitlements. What Powell feared most was permanence. For him, racial preferences were a short-term response to a pressing need."

At Harvard College in 1968 almost "half of alumni sons were being admitted"; this has declined in recent years to "approximately 40 percent of alumni children . . . against 14 percent of nonalumni applicants." This preference is justified by the claim that alumni are one of the "constituencies important to the college." It really exists to encourage alumni to be generous with their pocketbooks.

Affirmative action for designated race and ethnic categories in higher education is, at worst, patronizing, corrupting, and eventually demoralizing to its intended beneficiaries.

Preferential treatment of "legacies" in elite colleges and universities has received little criticism. It is a deplorable practice, more so than any preferential treatment of minorities and for which it provides perverse justification. Favoring legacies is a worse sin than favoring minorities because it lacks the altruistic, if misguided, intentions of affirmative action. It most directly discriminates against Asians, few of whom are legacies, and from whom it takes away places. Both forms of preference are violations of the universalistic and meritocratic standards that should be of bedrock importance to universities.

Presidents of major universities are among the most vocal Cassandras when contemplating the passing on of affirmative action. The president of the University of California, Chang-Lin Tien, has claimed that without affirmative action only about 2 percent of Berkeley undergraduates would be black. The president of the University of Texas at Austin, Robert A. Bergdahl, has lamented that without affirmative action only some 3 percent of those accepted to the university's law school would be black. Even if these estimates are on target, and they probably are, they should not be cause for alarm, nor a last-ditch argument for affirmative action in university admissions.

In a world without affirmative action, maybe only 2 percent of Berkeley undergraduates would be black, but maybe 15 percent of the undergraduates at nearby San Francisco State and San Jose State would be black. If only 3 percent of the entering students at the University of Texas Law School were black, maybe 10 percent of those at the state's somewhat less selective law school in Houston would be black. The most thoughtful reaction to such an unbalanced but discrimination-free system is, *So what!* The student—and faculty—composition of universities in our multiethnic country will always be unbalanced and in flux. Jews and Asians are more overrepresented in selective colleges than blacks and Hispanics are underrepresented. About a quarter of Ivy League undergraduates are Jews; over 40 percent of recent freshman classes at Berkeley and UCLA have been Asian. It took Italian-Americans six or seven decades after their heaviest immigration to this country in the first decade of this century to achieve parity with the general population in higher education.

Grades should decide admission

Only in America do we find the practice of admitting students to upper tier schools by using, in addition to academic criteria—grades and test scores—such dubious, presumptive, and downright irrelevant criteria as potential for leadership, character, personality, unusual life experiences, extracurricular activities, charitable activities, athletic, musical and other talents, special qualities allegedly revealed by written essays, plus letters of recommendation and interviews. If all this subjectivism and departure from objectively measurable academic merit is allowable in the name of achieving the elusive diversity and a balanced entering class, why not race and ethnicity too?

No fewer than twenty-three diverse people make up the admissions staff at Harvard. "We obviously want to get talented students from all backgrounds," says William R. Fitzsimmons, dean of admissions and financial aid at Harvard. He continues with a non sequitur, often unavoidable when attempting to defend what admissions people do: "One of the roles we've always played is to educate future leaders. Increasingly, African Americans are becoming more involved in the leadership of cities, states, and in Congress, and in that context we would be remiss if we weren't going out and getting talented people from every background." "To say that one person is more qualified for admission than another is tough to do," claims Karl M. Furstenberg, dean of admissions at Dartmouth.

There are no data anywhere to suggest that university admissions committees in highly selective institutions have any greater success in choosing successful entering classes, using all their subjective criteria, than if they went strictly by the numbers. Quite the contrary, since the publication more than four decades ago of Paul Meehl's *Clinical vs. Sta-*

tistical Prediction, the evidence is compellingly the other way: statistical prediction is better than clinical prediction in determining successful educational outcomes and successful job performance.

Universities, of all our institutions, should abhor discretionary and informal methods of selection when selection must be made.

Elite American colleges and universities would do well to admit students at all levels and in all programs solely on the basis of objective academic measures, just as is done in all western European universities except the colleges of Oxford and Cambridge. Universities, of all our institutions, should abhor discretionary and informal methods of selection when selection must be made. This includes law schools and medical schools. Law and medicine are both wide and varied fields in which there is scope for many different types of personality, many sorts of talent. Race and ethnicity—like being a so-called legacy or having had unusual life experiences or coming from Wyoming—should be irrelevant considerations.

Many people will argue that in such a coldly objective system narrow grade grubbers and successful test takers will beat out the erratic geniuses with wide interests, but less than stunning grades and test scores. But, again, *So what!* They can go to the University of Wisconsin instead of Yale.

This would be a great reform for American higher education. It would abolish the rampant subjectivism that now prevails in deciding who gains admittance to America's elite colleges, those that bestow extraneous status and career advantages.

A lottery system

The fairest, most efficient, and simplest system of admissions to our extraordinarily competitive colleges and universities would be a lottery system. Here is how it might work: A portion of an entering freshman class, say, a third, would be offered early admission only on the basis of grades and test scores. This means doing away even with interviews and letters of recommendation. These are the superbly qualified. The remaining two-thirds would be chosen by lottery from *all* those deemed qualified on the basis of the same measures used to choose the superbly qualified. These are the well qualified.

Not only would such a system remove the gratuitous discretion presently used in admissions to elite schools, it would make them a bit less elite, a move in the right direction for the world's most stratified system of higher education. It would produce a natural diversity instead of a contrived diversity.

A lottery system would not overcome the current over-representation of whites, most notably Jews and Asians, and the under-representation of blacks and Hispanics. *But it would lessen the over- and under-representation of the various groups because the net has been cast more widely.* More applicants are in the pool. Chance would be a factor as it is in life. No more would there be stigmatized "affirmative action babies," and no more would there be the excessive dropout rate of black and Hispanic students along with the sad consequences.

Below the super-selective institutions there is a tier of more modestly selective institutions for those who don't quite make it to the major leagues. And let it be put up in neon lights that most American colleges and universities are hardly selective at all. There is more than enough room for everybody.

If elite law schools adopted an analogous mode of admissions there would be no more insulting affirmative action mix-ups such as experienced by affirmative action baby Stephen L. Carter:

> As a senior at Stanford back in the mid-1970s, I applied to about half a dozen law schools. Yale, where I would ultimately enroll, came through fairly early with an acceptance. So did all but one of the others. The last school, Harvard, dawdled and dawdled. Finally, toward the end of the admission season, I received a letter of rejection. Then, within days, two different Harvard officials and a professor contacted me by telephone to apologize. They were quite frank in their explanation for the "error." I was told by one official that the school had initially rejected me because "we assumed from your record that you were white." (The words have always stuck in my mind, a tantalizing reminder of what is expected of me.) Suddenly coy, he went on to say that the school had obtained "additional information that should have been counted in your favor"—that is, Harvard had discovered the color of my skin. And if I had already made a deposit to confirm my decision to go elsewhere, well, that, I was told, would "not be allowed" to stand in my way should I choose to enroll at Harvard.

It is unfair to consider someone's race

It is subversive and dangerous practice to manipulate entrance requirements by race to achieve some allegedly desirable balance. Who is to decide what that balance should be? It is subversive because it is an assault on a merit-based ethic and on fairness to discrete individuals as opposed to a racial or ethnic category. This ethic is one of the fundamental values of modern democratic society, and it is being squeezed out by the new equality of group representation. Such social engineering is also socially dangerous because of its unintended consequences. Lowering entrance standards for blacks and Hispanics requires raising standards for whites and Asians. Within the selective institution this widens the gap between, on the one hand, whites and Asians, and blacks and Hispanics, on the other. In recent years the gap in SAT scores between whites and blacks has been an enormous 235 points at UCLA, 218 at Dartmouth, 206 at the University of Virginia, 171 at Stanford. Harvard has the lowest average difference in SAT scores among elite colleges, 95 points. The 1994 national gap in scores was 198 points, 217 for males and 181 for females. The implications of the gap between white and black undergraduates at Berkeley has been distressingly described by Vincent Sarich, who teaches anthropology there:

The gap between the two means [in SAT scores] has increased by more than 100 points in the past decade [1988 compared with 1978] (from 149 to 270), leading to a situation of minimal overlap (15 percent or less) between the two distributions. This current difference is equivalent to a four-year gap in academic preparation/achievement; in other words, the difference between a college junior and a high school junior.

The enormous, and growing, disparity tells us that, *on the average*, "minority" group students are not going to be competitive with "Asians" and "whites" at Berkeley. And whatever the faults of the SAT, or any standardized achievement test, we are being told the truth here. That truth is seen crudely in dropout figures, but is much more apparent to those of us who spend much of our time teaching undergraduates—in relative performance in the same classes, and in the lack of "minority" representation in our more demanding courses and majors. All this is depressing and most unfortunate, but nonetheless true—and, as you get more and more selective among "Asians" and "whites," the competitive gap necessarily increases. This is [*sic*] simple statistics, and nothing anyone here at Berkeley can do, short of admitting only those "Asians" and "whites" who score *below*, say, 1100, could change it.

An affirmative-action-induced division such as Sarich describes at Berkeley has become institutionalized in much of American higher education. But this will change for the better at the University of California if the regents' 1995 elimination of race- and gender-based affirmative action in admissions is actually carried out in practice.

In no institutional sector is the balkanization of our society seen more clearly than in the universities. In no sector will it be more difficult to phase out preferential affirmative action than in the universities. University of California Regent Ward Connerly made a shrewd assessment of why it will be so difficult to eliminate affirmative action in America's universities:

With each passing day it should be clear to us that our system of preferences [at UC and elsewhere] is becoming entrenched as it builds its own constituency to defend and sustain it as a permanent feature of public decisionmaking. . . . Our excessive preoccupation with race contributes to the racial divide, and nowhere is the art of race-consciousness practiced more fervently than on our university campuses.

10

Affirmative Action Policies Should Consider Class, Not Race

Richard D. Kahlenberg

Richard D. Kahlenberg is a senior fellow at the Century Foundation. He is both a vocal and longtime advocate of class-based affirmative action and is famous for his 1996 book, The Remedy: Class, Race, and Affirmative Action.

Traditional affirmative action, which uses race as a consideration in admission and hiring decisions, makes many Americans uncomfortable. Moreover, the "percent plans" implemented in states such as California, Florida, and Texas, whereby a certain percentage of top students graduating from each high school are guaranteed a place in the state university system, are also flawed in the eyes of many. A third alternative exists, however—basing affirmative action on economic class, not race. Although such a system would be expensive, as universities would have to provide financial aid to more candidates, it would ensure that, irrespective of race, students from poorly funded high schools in low-income areas would be able to receive a good education.

With the issue of affirmative action going before the Supreme Court tomorrow[1] for oral argument, the debate has come to focus almost entirely on two different approaches: racial preference plans of the kind used by the University of Michigan (and favored by Democrats and most of the business and education establishment) and the "top 10 percent" plan used by the University of Texas (which is supported by the Bush administration and a few other groups).[2] Unfortunately, little attention has

---

1. In 2003 the U.S. Supreme Court ruled in *Gratz v. Bollinger* that the University of Michigan's undergraduate admissions program, which used quotas, was unconstitutional. In *Grutter v. Bollinger*, the court ruled that the school's graduate program was constitutional.   2. By the percent plan, the top 10 or 15 percent of high school seniors from all schools in the state are automatically admitted to one or all of the state's universities.

been paid to a third alternative that has few political patrons but is supported by two-thirds of Americans: affirmative action for low-income students of all races.

Americans have always been uncomfortable with racial preference schemes such as that used at Michigan, which automatically adds 20 bonus points out of a possible 150 to every minority candidate's application. . . . In practice, affirmative action programs often benefit the most advantaged students of color. William Bowen and Derek Bok [former presidents of Princeton and Harvard] found that 86 percent of black students at the 28 elite universities they studied were from middle- or upper-status families.

[Sixty-five] percent of Americans support providing a preference to low-income students of all races.

But the Texas plan and similar plans in California and Florida, which automatically admit students in the tops of their high school classes irrespective of SAT scores, have their own problems. The concept has little independent justification beyond its ability to serve as a proxy for race, which makes the scheme legally vulnerable. The program's success is perversely contingent on the continued segregation of high schools and would produce far less racial diversity in states less segregated than Texas, California and Florida. By completely ignoring SAT and ACT scores, research shows, the program will result in large dropout rates at more selective colleges. And the programs won't work at graduate schools, where the affirmative action debate is especially intense.

Economic affirmative action

But there is a third way. A recent *Newsweek* poll found that 65 percent of Americans support providing a preference to low-income students of all races. Economic affirmative action is actively used in Texas, California and Florida, alongside the percentage plans, and has been at least as important in promoting racial diversity.

How would it work on a national scale? According to a study by Anthony Carnevale of the Educational Testing Service and Stephen Rose of ORC Macro [management consultancy], economic affirmative action at the nation's most selective 146 colleges would result in a 2-percentage-point decline in racial diversity and a 28-point increase in economic diversity. In a paper being published . . . by the Century Foundation [liberal think tank], Carnevale and Rose find that a race-blind economic affirmative action program would boost African American and Latino admissions from 4 percent (under a system of grades and test scores) to 10 percent, which is somewhat below the current 12 percent representation. The study's authors advocate combining race and class preferences in order to avoid the 2-point drop, but experience suggests most colleges will adopt economic affirmative action only when barred from using race.

While economic affirmative action, properly defined, would produce almost as much racial diversity as using race, it would produce far more economic diversity than racial affirmative action has. Today, even with extensive race-sensitive admissions policies, our selective colleges are economically segregated, a fact that supporters of affirmative action rarely acknowledge. Carnevale and Rose find that at the top 146 colleges, the lowest 25 percent of the population by economic status has just a 3 percent representation and the bottom economic half just a 10 percent representation. Meanwhile, the top economic quarter has a 74 percent representation. In other words, you are 25 times as likely to run into a wealthy student as a low-income student in our nation's elite colleges.

While universities routinely claim to give an admissions preference to disadvantaged students, in fact the representation of poor and working-class students would rise, not fall, if grades and test scores were the sole basis for admissions, the researchers find. Economic affirmative action would give the bottom half a representation of 38 percent. If diversity is defined broadly, to value differences in both economic and racial backgrounds—kids from trailer homes and ghettoes and barrios as well as suburban minorities—economic affirmative action would provide a large net gain in the total student diversity at elite colleges.

But would economic affirmative action jeopardize high standards? Carnevale and Rose find that under a system of economic preferences—which also would eliminate legacy and athletic preferences—graduation rates would climb slightly, from 86 percent today to almost 90 percent. One reason to be confident in their simulation is that economic affirmative action is not meant to be a challenge to merit but rather a better approximation of it. A 3.6 GPA and an SAT score of 1200 surely mean something more to a low-income, first-generation college applicant who attended terrible schools than to a student whose parents have graduate degrees and pay for the finest private schooling.

President [George W.] Bush's legal briefs mention economic affirmative action, but only in passing, perhaps because he thinks it smacks of "class warfare." But several members of the U.S. Supreme Court, including Justices Clarence Thomas, Antonin Scalia and Sandra Day O'Connor, have in the past endorsed economic affirmative action as an alternative to racial preferences. The irony is that it may be unelected conservative judges who finally pave the way for a popular plan benefiting America's low-income and working-class students.

11

Affirmative Action Policies Must Consider Race

Glenn C. Loury

Glenn C. Loury is a professor of economics at Boston University. Loury is the author of numerous books, including The Anatomy of Racial Inequality.

An important distinction to be drawn in the affirmative action debate is the difference between the means of affirmative action and its ends. Most people acknowledge that the ends of affirmative action—the achievement of racial diversity and a fairer distribution of resources in America—are desirable. However, they disagree as to the appropriate means to achieve this goal. Two competing means, or policies, that have been practiced include traditional race-based affirmative action and the percent plans, which admit the top 10 or 15 percent of all high school seniors to state universities. Although percent plans are *race-blind* (in that anyone can benefit from them), they are not *race-neutral*, because these plans ultimately aspire to achieve the same ends as traditional affirmative action by using different means. Ultimately, all affirmative action plans must strive to increase blacks' and Hispanics' access to higher education.

The clash over affirmative action is a clash between two deeply valid principles. The first is a procedural ideal: color-blindness. (Because race is a morally irrelevant trait, people should be treated without regard to it.) The second is a moral outcome: racial equality. (Since our history is marred by racial injustice, we should try to reduce racial inequalities in wealth and power.) In this week's [December 27, 1999] editorial ("Admitting Error"), *The New Republic*'s [TNR] editors are eloquent on the first point and blind to the second.

The alternatives to affirmative action being considered by states like Texas, California, and Florida are all about reconciling nonracial procedures with racially just outcomes. In Texas, for instance, the state would guarantee a place at any public university to students in the top ten per-

Glenn C. Loury, "TRB from Washington: Admit It," *The New Republic*, December 27, 1999. Copyright © 1999 by The New Republic, Inc. Reproduced by permission.

cent of every high school class, regardless of race. The editors are correct that this would lower admissions standards. But their predictions of educational havoc are hyperbolic. After all, in the years prior to enactment of the ten percent plan, more than 90 percent of Texas students in the top tenth of their high school classes who applied to the University of Texas at Austin were already being admitted.

More fundamentally, in their passion for racially neutral procedures, the editors blithely ignore racially unjust outcomes. Officials at elite public universities are not simply playing crude budget politics as they struggle to maintain black and Hispanic enrollments. They are trying, as best they can, to exercise responsible stewardship of multibillion-dollar state-funded educational philanthropies. Such institutions do not need diversity for their political viability alone. Promoting it also furthers a just social order. When the courts or voters demand that student admissions be color-blind, they are not insisting that universities abandon the effort to achieve racial diversity. Indeed, this is exactly the point of the new programs, programs that voters applaud and judges accept but which TNR's editors scorn.

Since our history is marred by racial injustice, we should try to reduce racial inequalities in wealth and power.

To oppose any decline in educational standards for the sake of racial diversity, as the editors in effect do, is to take an extreme position. It is to imply that race is not only illegitimate in admissions but—more fundamentally and disturbingly—irrelevant to the broader mission of America's public universities.

Color-blind versus color-neutral policies

To grasp the point, consider the following terminological distinction: If a selection criterion for college admissions can be applied regardless of the racial identity of applicants, call it "color-blind." On the other hand, if a selection criterion is chosen with no concern as to its impact on various racial groups, call it "color-neutral." The importance of this distinction becomes clear when one considers that both ameliorating the social disadvantage of minorities and exacerbating this disadvantage can be achieved with color-blind policies. Yet, intuitively, a color-blind policy explicitly intended to harm blacks could never be morally tolerable, while color-blind policies adopted to reduce racial inequality are commonplace and uncontroversial. For instance, while many object to the racial gerrymandering of electoral districts, most find acceptable the move from at-large to district-based elections, even when that shift is clearly made to get more blacks into office.

The ten percent plan in Texas and similar proposals in Florida and California are color-blind, in my terminology, but they are not color-neutral—and it's a good thing, too. These policies mainly benefit students with low test scores and good grades at less competitive high schools—

students who are disproportionately black and Hispanic. (And the legislative history in Texas shows clearly that this was the lawmakers' intent.) So, although the direct use of race in admissions decisions has been legally proscribed, Texas now uses a proxy for race calculated to achieve a similar result. Yet the reverse would be impossible. Had a color-blind admissions formula been proposed with the express intent of excluding black and Hispanic students, it would have been morally (and constitutionally) unacceptable.

Affirmative action redresses historical injustices

Why does the public denounce race-conscious admissions while enthusiastically endorsing race-blind efforts to achieve the same goals? Because Americans intuitively understand that reversing the effects of our history of white supremacy is good, while perpetuating those effects is evil. Hence, a college admissions formula cannot be judged solely by the instruments used to implement it. Most people of all races understand that we must also look at its consequences—primary among which is its impact on black and Hispanic enrollments. This is as it should be. In Texas, as elsewhere in the country, the key moral question is not race-blindness but race-neutrality.

This struggle among competing ideals is what the preference argument in college admissions is all about. When exclusive colleges and universities alter their admissions procedures to enroll more blacks and Hispanics (whether through affirmative action or ten percent plans), they tacitly and publicly confirm that racial equality is a fundamental concern, one worth paying a price for. And putting substantive racial equality high on our list of national goals has consequences beyond the ivory tower. It leads naturally, for example, to the idea that the end of formal discrimination against blacks in this post-civil-rights era should not foreclose a vigorous public discussion about racial justice. Critics of affirmative action, like the editors of this magazine, disagree. They argue that because an individual's race has no moral relevance, it is either wrong or unnecessary to formulate public purposes in racial terms.

> *Racial equality is a fundamental concern, one worth paying a price for.*

This argument is mistaken. Maintaining the legitimacy of public institutions by ensuring they serve all communities in the polity is prudent. And it is also just. To be sure, conveying to college students the ultimate moral irrelevance of race in our society is a deeply important pedagogical goal. Yet, ironically, attaining this goal may require functional attention by administrative personnel to the racial composition of the learning environment. Teaching that "not all blacks think alike" is much easier when there are enough blacks around to show their diversity of thought. Of course, students of all races should know this is true as a matter of principle. But in the real world it cannot be resolved simply by appealing to principle. People must experience diversity as a practical condition of their lives.

So my objection to the editors—and my defense of affirmative action and ten percent plans—rests on both practical and theoretical grounds. Many Americans are appalled at the prospect that the number of black students at elite college campuses might drop to two or three percent of the student body. They think this would be bad for the social and political health of our nation, and they think it would be morally wrong. I agree with them. But not everyone does. With an intense political campaign being mounted against affirmative action, much persuasion on this point will be needed. I suggest that we start by drawing a bright, clear distinction between the procedural morality of color-blindness and the historical morality of racial justice—a distinction whose importance TNR's editors unwittingly illustrate.

12

Affirmative Action Benefits American Society

Carol Moseley Braun

Carol Moseley Braun is an attorney and politician. She was a state representative for Illinois and an assistant U.S. attorney. From 1992 to 1998, she served as a U.S. senator before being dispatched to New Zealand as the U.S. ambassador. Moseley Braun also joined the race for president in 2004.

Affirmative action serves all elements of American society. Such programs make economic sense by fostering competition. By expanding the range of competitors to include members of historically underrepresented groups, affirmative action programs spur creativity, distribute opportunity more evenly, and ultimately benefit all by providing the best services at the most competitive prices.

W hen I was first appointed to the U.S. Senate Finance Committee, I encountered a little old lady in the hallway who congratulated me on becoming the first woman in history to receive a permanent seat on that powerful committee.

She then went on to say, while waving her hand rather mysteriously, "Now all will be revealed to you." I remember being sufficiently taken aback by her remark that my response was a half-hearted "thank you."

Being on the committee did not reveal "all" to me, but I did learn two things that are most often unspoken truths about finance. The first is that money is confidence. The second is that business runs on relationships.

Both of these have core relevance to the debate about affirmative action in contracting.

The global issue, of course, is what kind of civil society we want to have. Are we, as a nation, prepared to move in the direction of the noble intent of our Declaration of Independence, when it asserted that "We hold these truths to be self-evident, that all men are created equal," or are we still comfortable with the inherent hypocrisy that kept women and blacks and other non-whites from the "blessings of liberty"? Women could not vote until 1920, and for all intents and purposes, blacks weren't enfranchised throughout America until the 1960s. Power, control and economic opportunity have not yet "trickled down" to fully embrace the talent, capacity and potential that the majority population (e.g., women and minorities) has to bring to bear on business.

This is where the argument is joined regarding the fairness of affirmative action. Of course, the history makes clear that the exclusion of blacks and women was an accepted fact of life, supported by the law and all aspects of civil society. Those who oppose affirmative action . . . essentially argue that since they were not themselves part of that history, they are unfairly penalized. Some of those who favor affirmative action argue that the history is enough support for "leveling the playing field" on behalf of those who are the new competitors in the economic arena. Neither argument tells the whole story.

Affirmative action builds relationships throughout the community

Affirmative action serves the interests of the whole community—not only the women or minority contractors who may get an opportunity. Businesses that are owned and operated by women and minorities are statistically more likely to in turn give opportunity to other women and minorities, and so a ripple effect takes place. Women and black or Asian or Hispanic or other minorities leverage their opportunity by bringing in others who might not otherwise have a chance. Lawyers, suppliers, employees, managers; the entire panoply of economic actors becomes more diverse, more creative and often more productive because of the stirring of the competitive pot that occurs when the contracting of public dollars is spread out to a population that looks like America.

Breaking up the old boys' network, smashing the glass ceiling, opening doors, not only lets in new competitors but also new talent, new capacity and new ways of doing business. Affirmative action takes down barriers that sheltered white men from competition, by giving a boost to others who want to compete. It remains a competition. The minorities and women have to perform, but the track record has shown that they do perform, and that new businesses have sprung up because of affirmative action in contracting. On the contrary, where such efforts have been struck down, the disappearance of minority- and female-owned business speaks volumes.

The struggle is to get to the point where the relationships exist and the confidence abides in women and minorities to lead our business community. Indeed, the paucity of both in the boardrooms makes clear that many of the "old boys" are still more comfortable with one another than with racial or gender diversity. The survival of affirmative action creates hope that opportunity exists for those who have not yet had a chance to lead and that performance and talent will be rewarded. That hope keeps our society on a path toward progress and the fulfillment of the promise of the Declaration of Independence and the Constitution.

13

Affirmative Action Is Constitutional

Jamin B. Raskin

Jamin B. Raskin is a professor of constitutional law at the Washington College of Law at American University. Raskin was the former assistant attorney-general of the Commonwealth of Massachusetts. He is the author of We the Students: Supreme Court Cases for and About Students, *as well as* Overruling Democracy: The Supreme Court Versus the American People.

Although affirmative action was not an issue that the framers of the U.S. Constitution discussed, all evidence suggests they would have favored it. In the aftermath of the Civil War, for example, several important programs were established to actively and affirmatively attempt to help freed slaves achieve equality. Moreover, the Constitution was amended specifically to redress some of the injustices that resulted from slavery, such as poverty and lack of education. To be sure, there are compelling issues regarding affirmative action that must be debated, but its constitutionality should never be in question.

Whether you like affirmative action or despise it, all Americans ought to agree that the Supreme Court should only prohibit affirmative action in college admissions if the U.S. Constitution itself forbids it. After all, to strike down affirmative action in state-university admissions would constitute extraordinary interference by the high court with the rights of states to conduct their own affairs. The high court should undertake this sweeping activism against federalism only if the Constitution itself makes affirmative action unlawful.

This is an elementary point that, curiously, most "states'-rights" conservatives, in their rush to denounce the intolerable unfairness of "racial preferences," merrily skip over.

The Constitution, of course, says nothing about racial preferences, much less does it explicitly ban them. Thus, self-proclaimed "strict constructionists" on the high court must conclude that nothing in the letter of the Constitution compels the court to order the state of Michigan to alter its chosen college- and law-school admissions processes. The University of Michigan uses weighted preferences for racial minorities to undo the horrendous effects of its decades of exclusion and segregation, which amounted to nothing less than continuous affirmative action and racial quotas for white students.

Yet, the white plaintiffs today say Michigan's efforts to diversify its universities violate the equal-protection clause of the 14th Amendment.[1] But any justice who truly believes in "original intent" must reject this argument. Equal protection was added to the Constitution in 1868 by Radical Republicans to "secure 'to a race recently emancipated, a race that through many generations has been held in slavery, all the civil rights that the superior race enjoys,'" as Justice John M. Harlan argued in dissent in *Plessy v. Ferguson* [1896].

Constitutional precedents for affirmative action

The Congress that voted on equal protection wanted to topple the stubborn reign of white supremacy, not pretend it was not there. Congress designed Reconstruction in a specifically race-conscious way to uplift blacks and block the restoration of the slave masters. The so-called "Freedmen's Bureau" was set up to distribute free food and clothing not to all citizens but to blacks, and was authorized to sell 40-acre lots of confiscated land to them. The Radical Republican Congress also passed appropriations specifically to aid "destitute colored women and children." Thus, the members of Congress who wrote equal protection into the Constitution [and gave themselves power to enforce it] saw affirmative, race-conscious legislation as serving the 14th Amendment, not violating it.

In his famous dissent in *Plessy*, Harlan originated the "color-blindness" metaphor that now is the *cri de coeur* of conservatives who have been anything but color-blind for most of American history. But Harlan used that phrase to attack American apartheid and never once cast doubt on the validity of policies designed explicitly to benefit the black population. Moreover, in *Plessy*, he repeatedly invoked the 13th Amendment ban on slavery to explain why racial segregation was unlawful. "The arbitrary separation of citizens on the basis of race while they are on a public highway is a badge of servitude wholly inconsistent with the civil freedom and the equality before the law established by the Constitution."

Is affirmative action today a "badge of servitude" and slavery worn by whites? I know that it's not always easy being a white male but, come on guys, let's be serious. Guaranteeing a racially diverse freshmen class does not make us an oppressed minority.

Furthermore, even if you want to conscript Justice Harlan to the anti-affirmative-action cause a century later, his words only illuminate the severe moral limitations of the jurisprudence of color-blindness. For he saw color-blindness as perfectly compatible with the continuation of white supremacy. Consider the almost-always redacted words that precede his

---

1. In 2003 the U.S. Supreme Court ruled the University of Michigan's undergraduate admissions program unconstitutional in *Gratz v. Bollinger* while upholding the school's graduate admissions program in *Grutter v. Bollinger*.

famous dictum: "The white race deems itself to be the dominant race in this country. And so it is in prestige, in achievements, in education, in wealth and in power. So I doubt not, it will continue to be for all time, if it remains true to its great heritage and holds fast to the principles of constitutional liberty. But in view of the Constitution, in the eye of the law, there is in this country no superior, dominant, ruling class of citizens. There is no caste here. Our Constitution is color-blind."

> *The issue at hand simply is whether the Constitution itself bans affirmative action. Any serious reading of the Constitution tells us no.*

Thus, even if we [quite unreasonably] assume that Harlan's vision of color-blindness was intended to stop positive efforts such as affirmative action, such a vision is untenable because it only marries the pretense of legal neutrality with the reality of perpetual white supremacy. One might forgive Harlan—a former slave-owner and Know-Nothing crusader struggling to articulate racial liberalism—for the horrors of such a vision. As for his modern-day conservative enthusiasts, their polemical conversion to color-blindness seems too little, too late and all too convenient.

There may be good policy arguments against affirmative action, and conservatives certainly have been free to bring them before the Michigan Legislature. Some states, such as California, have debated affirmative action at state universities and dropped the policy. There is nothing compulsory about affirmative action, and its defenders certainly are not trying to use the courts to impose one admissions policy on all America. But there also is nothing forbidden about affirmative action. Yet, conservatives do want to use their 5–4 majority on the high court to clinch an issue judicially they cannot win democratically. With the Rehnquist court's invalidation of the Violence Against Women Act, the Gun-Free School Zones Act, the Religious Freedom Restoration Act, the Brady Handgun Control Act, parts of the Americans with Disabilities Act, majority-minority congressional districts and dozens of other federal and state laws, we clearly have entered an age of dangerous judicial activism and supremacy.

Affirmative action may be imperfect, but it is constitutional

Just because you feel affirmative action stigmatizes minorities or is unfair to whites or has outlived its social utility—all plausible but deeply controversial claims—simply does not make it unconstitutional. Today's conservatives are trying to inscribe their political preferences into constitutional law in a madcap way that is totally at odds with the text and original understanding of the Constitution, as well as settled law in the *Bakke* decision [1976].

Some policy arguments against affirmative action warrant consideration, especially the claim that it benefits only more-affluent minority students and distracts us from making much more sweeping change in our economically segregated education system. But, as a professor, I not only cherish but depend upon the intellectual, political, social, class and racial diversity of my classroom to teach effectively. I would not want to see any teacher or student have to give up that diversity. At the very least, there is a host of other changes that I would want to see implemented first to convince me that the critics of affirmative action are really seeking perfect meritocracy and not simply the destruction of the civil-rights movement.

First, we should abolish all alumni "legacy" preferences in public and private universities. These preferences, along with "donor" preferences, not only undermine the merit process but systematically favor whites, who are much more likely to have family ties at these schools. Second, we should abolish all geographic-distribution preferences. Like racial preferences, this factor advances only the much reviled "diversity" and does not reflect individual "merit." Third, all public and private universities that discriminated against blacks and other minorities in the past—which is to say almost all of them—should pay a huge one-time fee into a minority-student college tuition fund. Fourth, we should abolish property-tax-based systems of school funding and equalize public-school expenditures across rich and poor counties in America. Finally, we should make a massive social investment in rebuilding public schools across the nation and create world-class, preschool-education programs nationally.

These steps properly taken would show that the people campaigning against affirmative action truly believe in "equality of opportunity" and deeply despise all special preferences for undeserving applicants. I quickly would drop my support for affirmative action if we took these measures. But, with all due respect, can we really expect President George W. Bush—the self-proclaimed "C" student and legacy admittee to Yale College and Harvard Business School—to attack alumni preferences? Can we expect the conservatives who would divert untold billions of dollars from public schools to voucher programs suddenly to reinvest in our urban public schools? Can we expect a commitment to equal educational opportunity from conservatives such as Justice Clarence Thomas, whose career has embodied—shall we say, delicately—a paradoxical relationship to affirmative action?

In any event, these policy hypotheticals lead us far astray. The issue at hand simply is whether the Constitution itself bans affirmative action. Any serious reading of the Constitution tells us no. Conservatives used to know the difference between a constitutional question and a policy question. But that was long ago. The Rehnquist court, drunk on its own power, sorely will be tempted now to force all 50 states to drop any use of racial and ethnic diversity as a factor in higher-education admissions. The justices think they will be striking a blow for color-blindness, but they really will be striking a blow for Constitution-blindness.

Organizations to Contact

The editors have compiled the following list of organizations concerned with the issues debated in this book. The descriptions are derived from materials provided by the organizations. All have publications or information available for interested readers. The list was compiled on the date of publication of the present volume; names, addresses, phone and fax numbers, and e-mail addresses may change. Be aware that many organizations take several weeks or longer to respond to inquiries, so allow as much time as possible.

American Association for Affirmative Action (AAAA)
12100 Sunset Hills Rd., Suite 130, Reston, VA 20190
(800) 252-8952
e-mail: execoffice@affirmativeaction.org
Web site: www.affirmativeaction.org

This nonprofit organization is the professional body that advocates for affirmative action and equal opportunity throughout the country. The AAAA has organized an annual conference on affirmative action every year since its founding in 1974. Its comprehensive Web site contains information about the organization, including local contacts and regional information on affirmative action resources and news.

American Civil Liberties Union (ACLU)
125 Broad St., Eighteenth Floor, New York, NY 10004
(212) 549-2500 • fax: (212) 549-2646
Web site: www.aclu.org

Founded in 1920, the ACLU is an association of administrators and lawyers who ensure that the civil liberties of Americans (personal freedoms, freedom of the press, racial equality, and such) are not violated. They work primarily through legal means, handling individual cases of discrimination as well as working to uphold major legislation that ensures the protection of civil liberties on a societal level.

By Any Means Necessary (BAMN)
PO Box 12872, Berkeley, CA 94712
(313) 213-9779 • fax: (775) 255-2583
e-mail: letters@bamn.com • Web site: www.bamn.com

The Coalition to Defend Affirmative Action and Integration and Fight for Equality By Any Means Necessary (BAMN) was founded in Berkeley, California, in July 1995 in response to the high-level opposition to affirmative action in the University of California system. BAMN was formed to counteract the ending of affirmative action at several California institutions and to organize the struggle to prevent higher education from becoming resegregated.

Center for Individual Rights (CIR)
1233 Twentieth St. NW, Suite 30, Washington, DC 20036
(877) 426-2665 • fax: (202) 833-8410
e-mail: cir@cir-usa.org • Web site: www.cir-usa.org

The CIR is a nonprofit law firm dedicated to defending individual liberty. Politically conservative, the group is adamantly opposed to affirmative action and has encouraged individuals to sue on account of injustices suffered as a result of affirmative action. The CIR has provided legal counsel for Jennifer Gratz and Barbara Grutter, the plaintiffs in the two high-profile cases that reached the Supreme Court in 2003: *Gratz v. Bollinger* and *Grutter v. Bollinger.*

DiversityWeb
Association of American Colleges and Universities
1818 R St. NW, Washington, DC 20009
e-mail: diversityweb@aacu.org • Web site: www.diversityweb.org

DiversityWeb works to coordinate, connect, and advance diversity programs on university campuses through training programs and to help colleges and universities establish their own diversity initiatives. It is a joint project of the University of Maryland at College Park and the Association of American Colleges and Universities.

Heritage Foundation
214 Massachusetts Ave. NE, Washington, DC 20002
(800) 544-4843 • fax: (202) 544-6979
e-mail: pubs@heritage.org • Web site: www.heritage.org

This conservative think tank opposes affirmative action for women and minorities and favors limiting government involvement in areas such as education and social policy. Independently funded, the foundation publishes information on policy issues, as well as a quarterly journal, *Policy Review.*

Leadership Conference on Civil Rights (LCCR)
1629 K St. NW, Suite 1010, Washington, DC 20006
(202) 466-3311 • fax: (202) 466-3435
e-mail: comlccr@civilrights.org • Web site: www.civilrights.org

Founded in 1950, the LCCR is a coalition of various organizations, comprising more than 180 different groups committed to protecting civil rights in America. They manage the Leadership Conference on Civil Rights Educational Fund and run a comprehensive Web site.

National Association for the Advancement of Colored People (NAACP)
4805 Mt. Hope Dr., Baltimore, MD 21215
(877) NAACP-98 • 24-hour hotline: (410) 521-4939
e-mail: washingtonbureau@naacpnet.org • Web site: www.naacp.org

The NAACP is the nation's oldest organization established to protect the rights and liberties of African Americans. It was founded in 1909 by legendary activist and thinker W.E.B. Du Bois to fight the racism and discrimination against black Americans endemic to American society. The NAACP has traditionally fought for justice through legal and constitutional means, and its lawyers have argued in many of the key civil rights cases in the United States during the twentieth century. The NAACP also publishes *Crisis* magazine.

National Center for Policy Analysis (NCPA)
12655 N. Central Expy., Suite 720, Dallas, TX 75243-1739
(972) 386-6272 • fax: (972) 386-0924
e-mail: ncpa@ncpa.org • Web site: www.ncpa.org

The NCPA is a nonprofit, nonpartisan public policy research organization. It aims to develop and promote private alternatives to government regulation, using business and the private sector to solve problems that the government tries to deal with in areas such as affirmative action, health care, criminal justice, and the environment.

National Organization for Women (NOW)
733 Fifteenth St. NW, Second Floor, Washington, DC 20005
(202) 628-8669 • fax: (202) 785-8576
e-mail: now@now.org • Web site: www.now.org

NOW is a nonprofit organization supporting the rights and liberties of women and working to defend and advance women's rights. The organization advocates in women's issues such as abortion rights, economic equity, and violence against women. NOW lawyers also represent needy clients in cases where they have suffered discrimination.

Office of Federal Contract Compliance (OFCC)
U.S. Department of Labor
Frances Perkins Building
200 Constitution Ave. NW, Washington, DC 20210
(202) 693-7880 • fax: (202) 693-7888
e-mail: OFCC-Public@dol.gov • Web site: http://dol.gov/esa/ofccp

The OFCCP is a division of the U.S. Department of Labor's Employment Standard Administration, the office that enforces federal laws that federal contractors must adhere to policies of affirmative action in their hiring practices.

Office of Minorities in Higher Education (OMHE)
American Council on Education
One Dupont Circle NW, Washington, DC 20036
(202) 939-9395 • fax: (202) 833-5696
e-mail: omhe@ace.nche.edu
Web site: www.acenet.edu/programs/caree/home.cfm

The OMHE is a division of the American Council on Education (ACE). It aims to raise the number of minorities in higher education and focuses on issues in higher education that affect minority students and educators. ACE is the main coordinating body for institutions of higher education in the United States and seeks to provide leadership and resources for these educational institutions through research and advocacy.

Bibliography

Books

Steven M. Cahn	*The Affirmative Action Debate*, 2nd ed. New York: Routledge, 2002.
Linda Chavez	*An Unlikely Conservative: The Transformation of an Ex-Liberal*. New York: Basic Books, 2002.
Carl Cohen and James P. Sterba	*Affirmative Action and Racial Preference*. Oxford, UK: Oxford University Press, 2003.
Lee Cokorinos, Harold R. Tyle, and Theodore M. Shaw	*The Assault on Diversity: An Organized Challenge to Race and Gender Justice*. Lanham, MD: Rowman & Littlefield, 2003.
Ward Connerly	*Creating Equal: My Fight Against Racial Preferences*. San Francisco: Encounter, 2002.
Faye J. Crosby	*Sex, Race, and Merit: Debating Affirmative Action in Education and Employment*. Ann Arbor: University of Michigan Press, 2000.
Ronald Dworkin	*Sovereign Virtue: The Theory and Practice of Equality*. Cambridge, MA: Harvard University Press, 2002.
Andrea Guerrero	*Silence at Boalt Hall: The Dismantling of Affirmative Action*. Berkeley: University of California Press, 2002.
Robert A. Ibarra	*Beyond Affirmative Action: Reframing the Context of Higher Education*. Madison: University of Wisconsin Press, 2000.
Glenn C. Loury	*The Anatomy of Racial Inequality*. Cambridge, MA: Harvard University Press, 2002.
Alan Marzilli	*Affirmative Action*. Philadelphia: Chelsea House, 2004.
Fred L. Pincus	*Reverse Discrimination: Dismantling the Myth*. Boulder, CO: Lynne Rienner, 2003.
Kul B. Rai and John W. Critzer	*Affirmative Action and the University*. Omaha: University of Nebraska Press, 2000.
Peter H. Schuck	*Diversity in America: Keeping Government at a Safe Distance*. Cambridge, MA: Belknap Press of Harvard University Press, 2003.
Peter Wood	*Diversity: The Invention of a Concept*. San Francisco: Encounter, 2003.

Periodicals

Elizabeth Anderson	"Integration, Affirmative Action, and Strict Scrutiny," *NYU Law Review*, November 2002.

Perry Bacon Jr.	"How Much Diversity Do You Want from Me?" *Time*, July 7, 2003.
Trevor Corson	"The Hues of Affirmative Action," *Christian Science Monitor*, June 25, 2003.
Victor Goode	"Victor Goode Explains What's at Stake in the Conflict over Affirmative Action," *Color Lines*, Spring 2003.
Emmett Hogan	"Affirmative Action Harms Black Colleges," *Dartmouth Review*, May 7, 2001.
Harry J. Holzer and David Neumark	"What Does Affirmative Action Do?" *Industrial and Labor Relations Review*, January 2000.
Alan B. Krueger	"The Supreme Court Finds the 'Mushball Middle' on Affirmative Action," *New York Times*, July 24, 2003.
Stanley Kurtz	"Liberalism vs. Diversity: The High Stakes in the Supreme Court's Affirmative Action Decision," *Weekly Standard*, February 10, 2003.
Nicolas Lemann	"The Empathy Defense: Can the University of Michigan Save Affirmative Action?" *New Yorker*, December 18, 2000.
Orlando Patterson	"Affirmative Action: The Sequel," *New York Times*, June 22, 2003.
Ronald Roach	"Class-based Affirmative Action," *Black Issues in Higher Education*, June 19, 2003.
Stanley Rothman, Seymour Martin Lipset, and Neil Nevitte	"Racial Diversity Reconsidered," *Public Interest*, Spring 2003.
Abigail Thernstrom	"Affirmative Action: College Rulings Add Insult to Injury," *Los Angeles Times*, June 19, 2003.
Charles Whitaker	"Affirmative Action's Last Stand," *Ebony*, July 2001.

Index